SERIES EDITOR: LEE JOHNSON

OSPREY MILITARY ELITE SER

REDCAPS
BRITAIN'S PROVOST TROOPS AND MILITARY POLICE

WRITTEN AND ILLUSTRATED BY
MIKE CHAPPELL

OSPREY
MILITARY

First published in Great Britain in 1997 by OSPREY, a division of Reed Consumer Books Limited, Michelin House, 81 Fulham Road, London SW3 6RB and Auckland, Melbourne, Singapore and Toronto.

OSPREY
2nd Floor, Unit 6, Spring Gardens, Tinworth Street, Vauxhall, London SE11 5EH

ISBN 1 85532 670 1

Filmset in Great Britain
Printed through World Print Ltd., Hong Kong

Editor: Sharon van der Merwe
Design: Alan Hamp

For a catalogue of all books published by Osprey Military, please write to:
Osprey Marketing, Michelin House,
81 Fulham Road, London SW3 6RB

Author's Note

The author wishes to thank the staff of the Prince Consort's Library, Aldershot, for their help in the preparation of this title. Also to Sue Lyons of the RMP Museum for the provision of the photographs credited. The RMP have a fine museum at their Depot at Roussillon Barracks, Chichester. The displays trace the history of the RMP and its antecedents, and there is an interesting medal collection.

Publisher's Note

Readers may wish to study this title in conjunction with the following Osprey publications:

MAA 193 *The British Army on Campaign (1) 1816-1853*
MAA 196 *The British Army on Campaign (2) 1854-1856*
MAA 198 *The British Army on Campaign (3) 1856-1881*
MAA 201 *The British Army on Campaign (4) 1882-1902*
MAA 81 *The British Army 1914-18*

THE REDCAPS
BRITAIN'S PROVOST TROOPS
AND MILITARY POLICE

INTRODUCTION

The story of Britain's provost forces necessarily focuses attention on some of the less glorious episodes of British Army history. Had every British soldier over the centuries been an obedient and dutiful soul, there would have been no need for provost or military police. Sadly, armies – particularly in time of war – have always been home for the criminal, and the British Army has had its share of thieves and cut-throats, as well as its drunken and licentious element. Their excesses have not always been effectively dealt with by their own officers, which has resulted from time to time in breakdowns of discipline ranging from minor offences to serious crime. How these were contained, or dealt with, is the main theme of this book. The men who tamed the lawless are its subject.

Police forces are a fairly new concept in both civilian and military life. Sir Robert Peel established the Metropolitan Police in 1829 (after having set up a constabulary in Ireland) and in 1855 the British Army raised the first unit to bear the title of 'military police'. Prior to this, what would be called military policing today was carried out by provost marshals, officers and non-commissioned officers appointed to that office who went about helping with the maintenance of 'good order and military discipline'.

A probationer of the MMP in the late 1880s. He wears the uniform of his regiment, an Irish one judging by his 'harp' collar badges. Note the 'MMP' brassard, his good conduct chevrons (five years plus), his crossed–rifles marksmanship badge, 1885-pattern sword, and late 19th-century saddlery and equipment. (RMP Museum)

DISCIPLINE IN THE BRITISH ARMY

To be effective an army must be well-disciplined. Military discipline may be defined as the control or order exercised over an army; or, the rules or laws used to maintain this control; or the behaviour of soldiers subjected to these rules. From the days of Roman empire to the Gulf War, it has been axiomatic that a well-disciplined force will invariably defeat one with poor discipline. Good military discipline is therefore highly desirable; it can forge an army from the most unpromising human material, or turn the forces of a warrior race into an élite.

For more than three centuries the British Army has maintained standards of discipline that have been the envy of the world. This achievement is all the more remarkable considering that the profession of arms has, in that period, remained unpopular with the British. Until fairly recently discipline in the British Army was maintained by methods that – judged by the standards of today – were harsh and repressive. Perhaps they had to be. Before the 20th century the ranks of Britain's army were filled by that part of its population that the Duke of Wellington chose to describe as 'the scum of the earth'. Want, or the desire to escape gaol, compelled many to enlist. Others were enticed by trickery, or cash bounties that were frequently spent on glorious alcoholic binges. Few men sought the soldier's life from feelings of patriotism or a desire for adventure. Until the latter part of the 19th century most were illiterate, and most drank to an excess limited only by their paltry pay.

The methods used to turn such unpromising material into soldiers were frequently brutal. Their punishment when they transgressed was nearly always savage – and public. Invariably, troops were paraded to witness the application of the lash, or death by noose or firing squad, the reasoning being that the spectacle encouraged soldiers to obedience. Perhaps such barbarity was inevitable given the condition of the poor in England and Ireland in the 17th, 18th and early 19th centuries. This wretched portion of the population provided most of the recruits for the British Army, even though enlistment, 'going for a soldier', was an option of last resort. Habitual wrongdoers could expect repeated floggings. Wrongdoers on

Military Mounted Police at Aldershot, 1890s. Most of the NCOs wear the undress uniform of the MMP, but six of the senior NCOs wear full dress tunics – identifiable by their gold lace. The officer in the centre of the front row is Charles Broakes, Provost Marshal from 1885 to 1894. (Ray Westlake)

4

active service risked a death sentence. If the British Army did give up a bad soldier – usually to transportation to the convict colonies – they parted company with him after tattooing 'B.C.' for bad character, on his chest.

When Victorian reforms reduced the use of the lash, the need to ensure that there would be no soft options for miscreants led to the construction of military prisons. Life inside was unbelievably hard, serving the triple purpose of depriving a man of his liberty, subjecting him to a regime of backbreaking labour, and sending a message to those in the ranks calculated to discourage wrongdoing.

Only in recent years has compulsion been eliminated as a recruiter for the British Army. The ranks are no longer filled by conscription or men on the run from hunger, unemployment or civil gaols. Young men now volunteer for service because they freely choose the life of a soldier. For the first time in history, the British Army may give up on a bad soldier, and dispense with his services without the risk of a stream of others seeking discharge the same way. Wayward soldiers still find their way to Britain's last remaining military prison. But they go for correction and retraining, not for the punishment once meted out.

Military Law

The rules that a soldier must live by are codified in military law. Upon enlistment a British soldier becomes subject to military law as well as the civil law of his country. British military law is set out by an Army Act, Queen's Regulations for the Army, and various routinely issued orders and instructions. Early in his training a recruit will have the rudiments of military law

Military Foot Police, Malta, 1913. A splendid illustration of the 'undress' uniform worn at this time. The only colour alleviating the dark blue was red piping on the cuffs, shoulderstraps, trousers and cap crown. The RSM and RQMS have gold piping on their tunics, Royal cipher cap badges, and crown collar badges. (RMP Museum)

explained to him, just as centuries ago the Articles of War were read out to the British regiments raised in time of war. (The Articles of War were ordinances, usually issued by the monarch, for the governing of troops on active service. They set out offences and punishments – usually death or maiming. In various forms they existed from the time of the Norman Conquest. They had no application in peacetime prior to the establishment of a standing army.)

British military law evolved beyond these articles with the restoration of the monarchy in 1660, when regiments were raised that were to form Britain's first full-time, standing, regular army. Discipline in peacetime was lax, and it became necessary for parliament to pass a Mutiny Act in 1689; successive Mutiny Acts – with some intervals – were passed annually until 1878.

The inconvenience of a military code that was part Act of Parliament and part Articles of War was removed in 1879 with the passing of the Army Discipline and Regulation Act, and with the Army Acts of 1881 and subsequent years. These continued to set out military offences, and to decree the limits of punishment, powers of arrest and the powers of courts martial. As an example, offences in the early part of the 20th century included cowardice in the face of the enemy, mutiny and insubordination, desertion and absence without leave, disgraceful conduct, drunkenness, and the catch-all, 'conduct to the prejudice of good order and military discipline'.

At no time has the British soldier been left in doubt as to his position before military law, and if he was stupid enough to plead ignorance of it, he soon found out that his was an unacceptable plea!

An artist's impression of a Redcap controlling traffic 'between the firing line and the reserves'. The chaos at Loos, in 1915, may have been like this. (Ray Westlake)

PROVOST MARSHALS AND STAFF CORPS

The office of Provost Marshal is one of the most ancient in Britain and it is difficult to establish its origins with any certainty. But the duties of the Provost Marshal seem essentially the same today as they were in the 17th century: the maintenance of discipline, the prevention of crime, and the arrest and bringing to trial of soldiers offending military law.

What has changed are the powers of the Provost Marshal and his men. At the time of the English Civil War they could summarily punish offenders with floggings, 'riding the wooden horse', or running the gauntlet. Blasphemy was punished by boring a hole through the offender's tongue. There were 45 offences for which courts martial could award sentences of death, which were put into execution by the Provost Marshal. In the reign of Charles II each regiment had a Provost Marshal. Later, a Provost-Marshal General was appointed for the army, along with a Judge Advocate to administer military law.

At about this time a description of the duties of a Provost Marshal was published, stating him to be 'One unto whom is delivered the charge and keeping of all Delinquents and criminal offenders... He is first the greatest and principal gaoler of the Army... though some contemptuously have called him the Hangman... It is not lawful for the Under-Provosts to go at any time without halters, withs, or strangling cords of match, ever about them... The Provost Marshal hath the charge of all manner of tortures such as gyves, shackles, bolts, chains, belbowes, manacles, whips and the like and may by his ministers use them, either in the case of judgement or commandment from a Martial Court or otherwise upon unruliness at his own discretion: he is by his officers to see all places of execution prepared ... gallows, gibbets, scaffolds, pillories, stocks or strappadoes, or any other engine which is set up for terror and affright to such as behold it... The Provost Marshal must have an especial care to the keeping of the Peace, and... must prevent all Mutinies, Quarrels, and disorders... he shall ever have about him a guard of Under-Provosts and servants, who with short truncheons in their hands, ...shall enforce obedience to any lawful commandment which proceedeth from him, and having taken [offenders] in their actual transgressions, to commit them to prison, or the bolts, as the nature or evil example of the crime deserveth: for it is a duty expected at this officer's hands to be a ready suppresser of vice and disorder... The last duty of the Provost Marshal is [after the watch is set at night] to survey the Army, and see if it remains calm and still... if he hears in Sutler's cabins or other harbour any drunkards, tobacco-takers, or other unruly persons... he shall presently suppress them.'

Two corporals of the Military Mounted Police, 1917. The seated figure wears a pre-war, dark blue, forage cap with a red cover. He also wears the medal ribbons of the Meritorious Service Medal (awarded for gallantry from early 1917) and the Military Medal. Ray Westlake)

The same treatise described the Provost Marshal's duties as a supervisor of 'victuallers, viandors, merchants and others' plying their trades within the camp area. He set prices for their merchandise, and protected them from the 'insolence' of the soldiery. He checked weights and measures, and levied a charge of sixpence a week per stall – for the 'Lord Marshal'. He further saw to it that 'the Market Place of the Camp be once in two days swept and kept sweet and clean ... [and] that no man do the office of nature but in places convenient'.

These duties, so carefully set out by Francis Markham in 1662, changed little over the next hundred years or so, a period when mutiny and desertion were commonplace. (That of the Royal Regiment of Foot leading directly to the passing of the first Mutiny Act.) In 1739, for example, several independent companies of Scottish highlanders were formed into the regiment that later became known as the Black Watch. Their duties had been to patrol their native highlands as a form of gendarmerie, but in 1743 the regiment was ordered to London. When they were put on standby for overseas service, 112 men deserted and set out for Scotland, but were captured and tried for mutiny. The trials were arranged by Provost Marshal Dodd of the Savoy military prison in London (one of the earliest references to the use by Provost Marshals of a military prison). Of the death sentences meted out by the courts, three were executed by firing squad at the Tower of London, and the remainder commuted to transportation of one kind or another. With the dreadful means at their disposal, Provost Marshals and their men contained the worst excesses of British armies at home and abroad, in peace and in war, but their 'terror and affright' failed to impress Wellington's army of ruffians and cut-throats in the Peninsular War.

Wellington's Army

In 1809 Sir Arthur Wellesley (soon to be Viscount Wellington) commanded the British army in Portugal that was, over the next five years, to win for him fame, titles and a fortune. He would later write, 'We are an excellent Army on parade, an excellent one to fight, but we are worse than an enemy in a country.' Wellington realised that his army could never operate with success in Portugal and Spain until the 'irregularities and outrages committed by British troops' were curbed. He was scathing about the poor control exercised by regimental officers and NCOs over their troops, and felt that courts

A MMP lance-corporal examines a notice discouraging looting, Amiens, France, 1918. The NCO is not wearing a red cap-cover. (RMP Museum)

SOLDIERS
IT IS YOUR DUTY TO RESPECT THE PROPERTY OF OUR ALLIES. REMEMBER THAT THEIR HUSBANDS AND SONS ARE FIGHTING OUR COMMON ENEMY. WOULD YOU LIKE TO THINK THAT YOUR HOMES WERE BEING LOOTED WHILST YOU WERE AT THE FRONT?
PLAY THE GAME!

martial were ineffective in view of the readiness with which his soldiers committed perjury. He pressed for his command to have a regular Provost establishment on the lines of the French Gendarmerie Nationale and the Spanish Policia Militar, in place of the handful of Assistant Provosts, sergeants on ensigns' pay, that he so distrusted.

Wellington's main problem was the way in which his army indulged in plunder. Free for a moment from supervision, British soldiers straggled, looted, and drank to excess of the wine of the country, which they frequently stole. It was not only soldiers who were guilty of bouts of drunkenness in looted wine cellars. Their women indulged too, and were flogged by the Provosts when caught. (Such incidents led to the Peninsular soldiers' epithet of 'Bloody Provost'.) Soldiers caught in the act of plunder were often hanged by the Provosts, but the sight of their comrades swinging from limb or gibbet had little effect on the rest of the army. Most men felt they had a right to loot, and most officers did not bother to stop them.

Matters went from bad to worse after the battle of Ciudad Rodrigo in 1812 when the British forces gave themselves over to an orgy of looting, rape and drunkenness. The Provosts combined their forces but were unable to restore order for 24 hours. Eleven executions followed, but they had little effect on what took place weeks later after the storming of the town of Badajoz. For two days British, Spanish and Portuguese soldiers sacked the town and drank themselves insensible while part of the garrison was allowed to escape. On the third day Wellington had a gallows erected in the town and with it the Provost Marshal, his Assistant Provost Marshals and their Provost guards gradually restored order with summary hangings.

In early 1813 the authorities agreed to Wellington's request for the formation of a military police force, and the Cavalry Staff Corps, 'a Police Corps of two troops', was formed. Command went to Lt.Col. George Scovell, formerly of the 57th Regiment of Foot, and the ranks were filled by volunteers from mounted regiments. Shortly after formation the new corps had a strength of 11 officers and 180 men, and their duties included patrolling the line of march of British columns to prevent looting. Soldiers caught in the act were immediately hanged. It is interesting to note that men of the Cavalry Staff Corps wore the uniforms and equipment of the regiments from which they had come, but were instantly recognisable by the red scarves tied around their right shoulders. A forerunner perhaps of the red cap cover.

Despite the best efforts of the CSC and a much increased Provost Marshal's force, plunder and other crimes were never eradicated from

A Canadian infantryman attached to the Provost unit of his division (1st Canadian) for traffic duties. Note the collar badges of the 'tenth Canadians', the red patch of his division, 'Canada' shoulder titles, and his 'TC', Traffic Control, brassard. (Canadian official)

Wellington's Army. In June 1813, at Vittoria in northern Spain, the French army were defeated, but their pursuit was virtually abandoned when the British fell upon the enemy baggage train. The wagons contained a veritable Aladdin's cave of treasure: fortunes in coin from the 'military chest', the jewels and trappings of the court of Joseph Bonaparte, King of Spain, and the accumulated plunder brought out of Spain by the French and their collaborators. The victors went into a frenzy of looting. It was the biggest prize ever to fall into their hands, and they made the most of it, with officers 'contending for the … disgraceful gain'.

Wellington was furious at the conduct of his troops, later estimating that over 10,000 men had involved themselves in the sacking of the French train. Faced with such a massive breakdown in discipline the Provosts were powerless. (Most soldiers – and some officers – believed plunder to be their right by the ancient and unwritten rules of war, particularly after a town had been taken by storm. The legend of 'spoils of war' lived on through the sacking of the palaces at Delhi in 1857, and Peking in 1860, to the 'liberation' of Nazi booty in 1945 and the post-war exploitation of economies of defeated countries through black marketeering.)

When the army moved into southern France many soldiers felt it their privilege to take what they wanted in the homeland of their enemy. This attitude led Wellington to complain, 'There is no crime recorded in the Newgate Calendar that is not committed by these soldiers, who quit the ranks in search of plunder, and if the Staff Corps were three times as numerous and active as they are, they would not be sufficient either to prevent the mischief or detect those guilty of it.' One who was detected and brought to trial was the soldier hanged for rape, who thought that now he was in

CMP mounted detachment, Cairo, 1937, with perfectly turned-out men and horses. Note the pale cord breeches and black jack-boots worn only by the CMP at this time. The detachment is armed with .455 in. pistols and 1908-pattern cavalry swords. (RMP Museum)

France he could take his pleasure from any woman he fancied. The war came to an end with the capitulation of the French in April 1814 and the Peninsular army began to disband and disperse.

After Napoleon's escape from Elba, Wellington returned to the Continent in command of an army which had been raised by the nations allied against Bonaparte. Once more, the Provosts were hard put to contain plundering, flogging any soldier found away from his regiment without proper authority. (This practice offended the sensibilities of at least one observer who recorded his outrage. One wonders what his feelings might have been if he had been the victim of the men he pitied.) On 18 June 1815, the day of Waterloo, Lt.Col. Scovell received orders to reform the Cavalry Staff Corps by recruiting as many former members as he could find, and by taking three men, preferably French-speaking, from each cavalry regiment. (Contemporary accounts refer to the unit as the 'Mounted Staff Corps' and the 'Gendarmerie Anglaise'.) The Corps remained on provost duties on the continent until 1818. During the Allied occupation of Paris its citizens were spared the worst attentions of the armies which were camped outside the city by the Provost guards who were posted on all the points of entry. No soldier could enter Paris without a pass.

Having fought for so long to have a Cavalry Staff Corps, Wellington authorised extra pay for troopers of the CSC (latterly one franc – or tenpence per day). But he refused to contest a peacetime cut in this allowance, instead allowing his 'Gendarmerie Anglaise' to fade away to disbandment. The British Army was to have no regular military police unit, other than the troops of the Provost Marshal, for another 36 years.

Posed for the camera – and therefor amusing – a collision between a Rifle Brigade truck and a Gloucestershire Regiment staff car, late 1930s. Note the waterproof clothing of the CMP motorcyclist, and the fact that puttees were no longer worn by Redcaps in service dress. (RMP Museum)

VICTORIAN MILITARY DISCIPLINE

The Mounted Staff Corps

Following the outbreak of war with Russia in 1854, a number of administrative corps were raised for the support of the British forces in the Crimea. One of them was a Mounted Staff Corps, to operate under the Provost Marshal. The 50 troopers of the MSC came from the Royal Irish Constabulary and the Metropolitan Police, and arrived at the base of Balaclava 'in fanciful helmet, red tunic braided with black cord … looking very much as if they… were the advance guard of some equestrian troop coming to open a circus'.

The dead hand of Wellington still lay heavily upon the British Army, for it was Sir George Scovell (now a lieutenant-general) who had drawn up the brief for the MSC, based – one supposes – on his experiences with the Cavalry Staff Corps in the Peninsula. Unfortunately Lord Raglan – the commander in the Crimea and yet another of Wellington's protégés – showed little interest in the MSC and they spent their time policing the harbour of Balaclava and protecting the supplies, moving from there to the British lines around Sevastopol. Within weeks the dreadful conditions and climate of the Crimean winter had reduced the force to 28 men and a handful of horses, and by the autumn of 1855 the survivors, who had been relegated to the conveyance of despatches, were disbanded. They went unmourned by most, and were certainly not missed by the Provost Marshal

CMP motorcyclists, 1941. Note their fibre helmets and waterproof suits. (RMP Museum)

Trainees undergoing instruction in traffic control, CMP Depot, Mytchett, 1941. A hutted camp, Mytchett was but one of the headquarters used by the Redcaps in the vicinity of Aldershot until the move to the present depot at Chichester. (RMP Museum)

and his men who were busy keeping order among the soldiers, sailors and civil labourers of many nations. The lash was used to punish them all, and the brutal treatment of civilians led to much resentment.

The Military Mounted Police

As the men of the ill-fated Mounted Staff Corps were serving out their last days in the Crimea, a military police force was raised for the 'Cantonment of Aldershot'. In early 1855 an encampment of tents and huts, that would one day grow into a great military town, had just become established to the west of the Hampshire village of Aldershot. Almost immediately the boundary of the camp became a shanty town to rival the main street of any wild-west town of the time. Competing for the custom of soldiers and construction workers were ale-tents, grog-shops, dance halls and brothels, while some of the first permanent buildings were those of 'soldiers' homes' set up by the churches to offer Tommy Atkins an alternative to vice and sin. Units from the regular army and the Militia came to this 'camp of exercise' to carry out field exercises on the nearby common and to shoot on the ranges. The Militia had been embodied during the Crimean War and had a poor disciplinary record (there had recently been a series of Militia riots). A military police force was raised for the cantonment, both to patrol the camp and to staff the prison within it. (The latter was a series of huts built to accommodate over 200 prisoners. A 12-foot stockade fenced in the compound, which was built in the North Camp.)

In July 1855 21 NCOs and men drawn from the 2nd Dragoon Guards, 3rd Light Dragoons, 15th Hussars and 17th Hussars took up duty 'to be employed as a Corps of Mounted Police for the preservation of Good Order in the camp at Aldershot, and for the protection of the inhabitants of the neighbourhood'. As well as the Military Mounted Police (MMP), each brigade in the cantonment eventually had its own Assistant Provost Marshal, each unit its Regimental Police (RP), while units contributed soldiers for a garrison military police force (GMP) which worked under the guidance of the MMP.

This force was often needed to deal with misbehaving soldiery, both in barracks and in the town. The combination of strong drink, loose women, and fierce, tribal, inter-regimental rivalry often brought about violence, sometimes on a grand scale. One of the worst incidents occurred in 1893. 'The Battle of Badajoz Barracks' was fought between the 20th Hussars and the Scottish Rifles (Cameronians). It began after a brawl in the town, in which a hussar was badly beaten by a group of Scotsmen. For two nights the Hussars went on the rampage, attacking Badajoz Barracks, the Scottish Rifles' accommodation, and searching the bars in downtown Aldershot for the men who had put their comrade in hospital. On the

CMP traffic control signs, Normandy, 1944. (RMP Museum)

second night the civilians of Aldershot turned out in crowds to watch the spectacle as the Provost services and the resources of an infantry brigade and two regiments of cavalry attempted to restrain the rioters. Matters were brought under control when the 20th Hussars were marched out of town and put 'under canvas', while the Scottish Rifles were moved to a barracks in North Camp. Courts martial dealt out hefty sentences in the wake of the riot, and the ringleaders found themselves behind the walls of the infamous 'glasshouse', the military prison built in North Camp in 1870 to replace the original stockade and huts.

From its foundation the MMP grew in numbers and in the scope of its duties. A detachment went to Egypt in 1882, and was present at the battle of Tel-el-Kebir. In the aftermath of the battle the MMP and Provost Marshal's men attempted to control the looting of the enemy camp, eventually forcing the transgressors to hand in much of the booty. In the same year a Military Foot Police was formed in Cairo, establishing a second corps of military police. The MMP and the MFP – frequently referred to as a 'corps of Military Police' – expanded as detachments were formed to police garrisons at home and abroad. In 1877 the MMP became established as a permanent corps, the MFP followed in 1885. From 1887 all MP private soldiers were given the rank of lance-corporal.

The Army Act of 1879 removed from Provost Marshals the power to inflict summary punishment on soldiers. Henceforth, all men had to be brought before a court to decide their guilt or innocence of charges. As the 19th century drew to a close, the power and influence of the MMP and the MFP grew so that the corps became the most important of the assets available to Provost Marshals. Volunteers for service as military policemen had to be of exemplary military character, to have served in their regiments for at least four years, and be prepared to undergo periods of probationary service before being taken on as a fully-fledged member of the MMP or MFP.

Provost duties still involved enforcing discipline, although on training and campaign military police also had traffic control and lines of communication duties, an aspect of military policing that was to burgeon in the wars of the 20th century.

THE EARLY 20TH CENTURY

In the early years of the 20th century the Provost Marshals of British Army garrisons at home and abroad employed military policemen of the MMP and the MFP almost exclusively in the enforcement of discipline. In 1901, military prisons, previously the province of pensioned NCOs under governors who were retired officers, became the responsibility of a Military Prison Staff Corps, a body of serving soldiers. (Each garrison also had a Provost Prison for soldiers undergoing sentences of up to 42 days, which was run by the Provost Marshal and his men.) It was some years before military prisons were run wholly by the MPSC, who implemented the military prison reforms then underway. They were long overdue.

For most of the 19th century military prisoners wore grey prison uniforms and shaven heads as they toiled at 'shot drill', breaking rock into gravel, and

A CMP motorcyclist putting up a traffic sign, Germany, 1945. Note his helmet, raincoat and boots, issued only to motorcyclists, and his Mark III 9 mm Sten machine-carbine. (RMP Museum)

Berlin, 1945. With obvious pride, two 'Redcaps' of the 7th Armoured Division – the famous 'desert rats' – put up a single sign recording the journey of their formation from north Africa to Berlin. (RMP Museum)

picking oakum from old rope. Misbehaviour was punished by a bread-and-water diet, isolation in darkened cells, and up to 25 lashes with the birch or cat-o'-nine-tails. Silence was enforced at all times. Diet was monotonous: breakfast was bread and cocoa; dinner, bread, boiled meat and onion; supper, bread and porridge. On Sunday there was suet pudding. From 1901, the new system allowed the soldier to wear military uniform, to drill, practise musketry, gymnastics, and other soldierly skills. Prisoners worked in shops making equipment such as harnesses, but shot-drill and oakum-picking remained for several more years. In 1906 alterations in nomenclature changed the Corps title to Military Provost Staff Corps, and prisons into either 'Military Prisons' or 'Detention Barracks'. Cells were to be termed 'detention rooms'. Whatever the terminology, life in institutions such as the Aldershot 'Glasshouse' was no bed of roses. Punishment was still the order of the day, and correction was a long way off in the future

The Boer War

On the outbreak of war with the Boer republics in 1899, nearly all Britain's 300 military policemen were dispatched to South Africa. They went from MP units in the United Kingdom, Malta and Egypt, to be employed under the Provost Marshal on a wide range of duties over and above their peace-time tasks. These included the supervision of civil police forces; the care of prisoners of war in transit to prisons and camps; the provision of guards for

A CMP mounted detachment on patrol, Vienna, 1946. The horses are former German mounts, as are the saddles and bridles. (RMP Museum)

'important places'; the issue of permits and passes, and the confiscation of arms and ammunition.

When the British took the war into the Boer republics, the enemy responded by waging a hit-and-run guerrilla war. Ranging the countryside on sturdy ponies, the Boer 'commandos' proved difficult to defeat until Lord Kitchener devised new tactics which included destroying farms supplying the enemy, and the detention of Boer families in 'concentration camps'. The first move led to an outbreak of ill-discipline and looting, unofficially condoned, which the Provost Marshal and his forces found all but impossible to regulate. The situation was exacerbated by the conduct of the Boers, who were forced to loot to survive, and by the rumour that Kitchener had said that his troops should 'loot like mad'.

Blame for much of the subsequent misconduct fell upon the 'Colonials', mounted units raised in South Africa and the white colonies. Serving in such a unit, the Bushveldt Carbineers, was Lt. Harry Morant, convicted by a court martial in 1902 of the murder of Boer prisoners. (His story was dramatised in the Australian film, *Breaker Morant*.) The court tried Morant and four other officers of the Bushveldt Carbineers on 16 charges of murder, but the unit was thought to have murdered at least 6 other Boers, two of their own men, and an unknown number of blacks. Morant and another Australian officer were shot by firing squad. A third Australian officer was sentenced to life imprisonment. Their partial defence had been that they had been told that Lord Kitchener himself had ordered Boer prisoners to be shot. The court martial took the view that the Carbineers' duty had been to hand them over to the military police for escort to a prison camp.

The concentration camps into which Boer families were placed were not well-run, and disease and malnutrition caused the subsequent deaths of many thousands of internees – resulting in bitterness felt to this day. For

Japan, late 1940s. A British Redcap lance-corporal and a CMP (India) NCO patrol on Matchless 350 cc motorcycles. (RMP Museum)

part of their existence the camps were under military control, but at least one Provost Marshal's humane treatment of those in his care has gone on record.

The British Army learnt many lessons from the Boer War of 1899–1902, and subsequently improved its performance with new weapons, equipment and tactical doctrine. The Army ignored, however, the Adjutant General's recommendation that the duties of the Provost Marshal and the forces under his command should be clearly defined. This oversight was to put Provost services at a severe disadvantage in the great conflict that was to come.

RMP guard dogs and their handlers on parade, Tripoli, North Africa, 1950. Note the khaki drill uniforms, and the gauntlets of the dog handlers. (RMP Museum)

1914–18 THE GREAT WAR

Of the monarchs, statesmen and high political figures who committed their nations to the 'Great European War' in August 1914, none expected it to last for more than a few weeks. Britain mobilised her army (her 'contemptible little army', as the Germans dubbed it) including the 761 officers and men of the corps of military police. This figure included 253 reservists recalled to the colours, but it soon became obvious that many more military policemen were going to be needed and that the peacetime standards of the MMP and the MFP were going to have to be lowered.

Within months of its outbreak the war had developed into an entrenched deadlock in Belgium and France, with other theatres of war established as nations joined the fight, or as German overseas possessions were fought for. Britain was forced to massively expand the army, and in the atmosphere of crisis that prevailed, military police recruiting procedures had to be drastically revised. Probation became a thing of the past. Many old soldiers were enlisted directly from civil life, as were civil policemen, and units of infantry and cavalry were transferred en bloc. The practice of temporarily 'attaching' men, or complete units, for police duties continued.

At first each divisional establishment included an Assistant Provost Marshal (usually a captain) and 25 NCOs of the MMP. Corps headquarters had a small detachment of MFP men. The APMs on lines of communications duties had even fewer men. As far as provost duties were concerned, no instructions existed as to what these might be, and they had to be defined and acted on as they became apparent. In France these mainly included the manning of 'stragglers' posts', traffic control, dealing with crime committed by British soldiers, the control of civilians within the battle area, handling prisoners of war, and patrolling rear areas and ports. Of these, perhaps the operation of stragglers' posts has become the least understood, giving rise to the legend of the Redcap, pistol in hand, forcing shell-shocked Tommies forward to certain death. The facts paint an entirely different picture. Stragglers' posts, or battle-stops, as they were sometimes called, were collecting points behind the front lines where prisoners of war were taken over from the infantry, runners and message-carriers were checked and directed, walking wounded from Regimental Aid Posts were directed to casualty collecting stations for evacuation, and 'stragglers' were dealt with. This last-named duty involved halting soldiers who were obviously neither casualties, signallers or runners, re-arming and equipping them if necessary, and sending them forward to rejoin their units, individually or in groups. With so few MMP or MFP men available, this type of work was mostly done by 'trench police' or 'battle police', men from a division's cavalry squadron or cyclist company, regimental police or corps cavalry, who also directed traffic in communication trenches. All worked under the

Singapore, 1951. An RMP Land-Rover detachment practise 'riot drills'. They are armed with .38 in pistols and Mark V 9 mm Sten machine-carbines, and their uniforms are jungle green. (RMP Museum)

direction of the divisional APM. Later in the war, a typical division in the line employed over 250 officers and men on provost duties within its area. They manned four straggler posts, provided an MP presence at the casualty collection post, operated various road traffic control posts and a number of mobile traffic patrols.

The importance of traffic control in the battle area was evident from the start of the war, but a planned approach to the problem of traffic did not emerge for some time. At first, divisional provost troops attended to the needs of their own formation, but this attitude frequently led to delays. Improvements were made, but not in time to prevent a serious traffic control problem at the battle of Loos in September 1915. After the start of the battle, two divisions, the 21st and the 24th, were called forward from reserve to exploit a breach in the enemy's line. Their approach march has been described by one commentator as like trying 'to push the Lord Mayor's procession through the streets of London without clearing the route or holding up the traffic'. The infantry of the two divisions arrived at the battle late and exhausted, and their attack failed. In the wake of the disaster the problems of traffic control were properly tackled and corrected. From then on, standards were such that it was said, 'the afterwards excellent system of traffic control was evolved as a result of the lessons of that day'.

Absenteeism and desertion became an increasing problem as the war progressed. It was the duty of military policemen to apprehend deserters and hold them for trial by court martial. Much has been written about the British soldiers of the Great War who suffered death by firing squad for the crimes of cowardice or desertion. More than 3,000 sentences of death were passed by British courts martial between 1914 and 1920, of which 346 were

Korea, 1953. Redcaps of the 1st Commonwealth Division ride in a Jeep. Note the markings on the vehicle. (RMP Museum)

carried out; 266 were for desertion, 18 for cowardice, 37 for murder, seven for quitting post, three for mutiny, two for sleeping while a sentry, six for striking a superior officer, five for disobedience and two for casting away arms. Many of those shot were under suspended sentences of death and had re-offended. Against these figures should be balanced those of the 702,410 officers and men of the British forces who were killed in action. Assistant Provost Marshals and their men had the grim duty of supervising the executions of men sentenced to death. They were not required to furnish firing squads. Many deserters chose to disappear when their units were out of the line, attempting to get aboard a ship at one of the French ports. Others set up house with French women they had befriended.

They, and other serious offenders, if not sentenced to death, rapidly found their way to Field Punishment Centres or Military Prisons. These were run by men of the MPSC and by military policemen, while Provost Marshals had the supervision of the FPCs. Little remains in the way of records of these institutions other than the fact that they were run as 'worse-options' to conditions in the front line. The court martial on charges of mutiny of a number of soldiers undergoing sentence at the FPC at Blargies, France, gives us an insight into the regime being operated. In 1916 Australian soldiers undergoing sentence at Blargies had mutinied, and some of their grievances were attended to. Two days later 67 British SUS (Soldiers Undergoing Sentence) confined in leg-irons refused to parade as a protest against their shackling and their dietary punishment. At their trials seven ringleaders produced further complaints, objecting to being kept in a verminous state, being tied to poles until they fainted, being blindfolded and being assaulted by the staff. The court listened to the Director of Military Prisons in the Field state that this treatment was acceptable, and then passed out six sentences of death. One was carried out and the rest commuted to terms of imprisonment. Compared to such conditions the 'crucifixion' Field Punishment (the prisoner being tied, spreadeagled to the wheel of a wagon) recorded as being carried out in units seems almost benign.

During the First World War 'Redcap' or 'Cherrynob' became the terms applied by British soldiers to any military policeman. (The epithet referred

North Africa, 1950. A photograph illustrating that 'close protection' is not a recent innovation. RMP personnel and Royal Signals wireless operators stand in front of the escort vehicles for Field Marshal Viscount Montgomery, during one of his visits to Libya. (Private collection)

to the red cap cover which had been taken into use before the war to distinguish an MP on duty, when the blue uniform then worn resembled that of a civilian policeman. The practice of wearing red cap covers continued with khaki service dress, but was only worn by men of the MMP and MFP.) Not all the men attached for provost duties were as efficient as the regular Redcaps, and their behaviour at times fell short of the standards of the corps. In September 1917, the base camp at Etaples was a hot-bed of discontent and potential mutiny. Matters came to a head over the arrest by the camp police (in some reports, the military police) of a New Zealand gunner. A noisy and violent crowd of between 3,000 and 4,000 men gathered at the police guardroom, and in the altercation which followed Pte. Reeve of the camp police fired a number of shots from a revolver. One bullet mortally wounded a Cpl. Wood of the 4th Gordons, and another hit a Frenchwoman bystander. A riot developed, during which L/Cpl. Jesse Short committed acts of incitement for which he was arrested, tried, and subsequently shot. For several days the base was in turmoil until the Provost Marshal of the BEF with a force of cavalry, machine gunners, battalions of infantry and the provost resources of the area managed to bring the mutiny under control. The original camp police were replaced and matters returned to normal. (Pte. Reeve, the camp policeman who had sparked off the mutiny by drawing and firing his revolver, was tried for manslaughter and sentenced to one year's hard labour.)

A corporal of the WRAC Provost, Singapore, 1950s. Note her service dress cap – with WRAC badge and red cover – 'Provost' titles, Singapore District formation sign, and RMP badge on her left breast. (RMP Museum)

Despite such incidents, discipline in the British Expeditionary Force in France, and in the armies at home and in other overseas theatres was properly maintained throughout the war. The British suffered no serious breakdown of discipline like that in the French Army in 1917, and this was due

Kenya, 1950s. HRH the Duke of Gloucester greets a sergeant of the RMP. Note the 'crossed pangas' formation signs of East Africa Command, worn by the sergeant and by the Askari of the King's African Rifles. (RMP Museum)

in no small measure to the efforts of provost forces. By the end of the war the strength of the forces under the control of the Provost Marshal of the BEF had grown to over 12,000 officers and men, while it has been reckoned that over 25,000 men served in a provost role during the war. Their achievements had a particular cost. The pre-war soldiers' respect for the Redcap had plummeted by 1918 to an all-time low, particularly within the ranks of the 'poor bloody infantry', who saw the military policemen as the instrument of a brutal regime which had sent them into the line again and again, and had savagely punished their weaker comrades. The constant Redcap presence, in the line and out, particularly that of a minority of over-zealous or bullying MPs, exacerbated the ill-feeling. This was a great pity, for the legend of the brutal Redcap devalued the achievements of British Provost forces, who had risen to the challenges of the war and, in the word of Field-Marshal Sir Douglas Haig, Commander-in-Chief of the BEF, 'In the battle zone, where frequently they had to do duty in exposed positions under heavy fire and suffered severe casualties, the military police solved an important part of the problem of traffic control. In back areas their vigilance and zeal have largely contributed to the good relations maintained between our troops and the civilian population.'

In December 1918 a military police motorcyclist had the honour to be the first British soldier to cross the Rhine in the occupation of Cologne. It was entirely fitting that a Redcap should lead the way for a victorious 'British Army of the Rhine'.

British, Canadians and Australians of the SIB, Japan, 1955. (RMP Museum)

1918–1939 THE INTER-WAR YEARS

In the two decades that followed the Armistice of 1918, Britain's provost troops underwent a great deal of reorganisation, much of it as a result of experience gained in the Great War.

In February 1926 the Military Mounted Police and the Military Foot Police were amalgamated to form a single corps under the title, the Corps of Military Police, or CMP. The 1930s, in particular, were a time of change for the new corps. Provost companies were formed (both in the Regular and the Territorial Armies), direct enlistment was authorised, reservists from the Brigade of Guards who had followed careers as civilian policemen were taken on as CMP reservists, and a supplementary reserve was formed. (A Field Security Wing was formed in 1937, but this became part of the newly formed Intelligence Corps in 1940.) Mechanisation – the change from animal transport to mechanical transport – went ahead, and, perhaps most important of all, the role of the CMP was clearly defined in *The Manual of the Corps of Military Police*, published in 1936.

By 1939, the Corps of Military Police was respected and valued by the rest of the British Army. Its reputation had been fully restored from the low esteem in which the Great War Redcaps had been held. The authority of the CMP went unchallenged, and in most units it was considered a disgrace for a soldier to appear before his commanding officer on a 'Redcap charge'.

RMP dog and handler, Kenya, 1950s. (RMP Museum)

No. 200 Provost Company on parade, Singapore, 1956. (RMP Museum)

By their deportment and conduct the men of the CMP usually presented a stern image. But there could, at times, be humour for the onlooker – even slapstick – in the way they tackled their duties. Between the wars, the Aldershot Military Police guardroom stood facing the civil part of the town, at the bottom of Gun Hill. (And, incidentally, a few yards from the civilian police station.) The 'Redcap lockup' was a highly polished building with a pair of ancient cannon decorating its forecourt. In the road in front of this splendour stood a public urinal, and immediately opposite the convenience were situated several of the hundred-or-so public houses that catered to the collective thirst of the garrison. On busy, boisterous nights, when the guardroom cells were full, any overflow might find themselves chained to the cannons. On really busy nights the Redcaps were known to resort to handcuffing drunken soldiery to the railings of the urinal!

1939–1945 THE SECOND WORLD WAR

On the outbreak of war the strength of the CMP stood at little more than that of the MMP and MFP of 1914. Mobilisation, however, brought the strength of the Corps of Military Police up to 3,500 officers and men. (By 1945 the CMP had expanded to over 50,000 men, an indication of the importance of the role of the CMP over these years.)

Some of the first CMP units to experience action were those which crossed to France with the British Expeditionary Force in September 1939.

A 'passing-out' parade to mark the end of training, of a group of RMP NCOs, August 1959. The ceremony was photographed at Inkerman Barracks, Woking, then the Depot of the RMP. In 1959 depots were taking in the last of the National Servicemen. (RMP Museum)

26

In the chaos of evacuation during the fall of France in May 1940, it was often the CMP straggler post or even a solitary Redcap who kept order and maintained discipline. Many Dunkirk survivors vividly remember the CMP sergeants whose authority was exercised to such good effect on the crowded beaches.

The evacuation was followed by the aerial Battle of Britain, after which the threat of an invasion of England diminished slowly. The British Isles became the base from which the assault on occupied Europe was to be launched, and in the preparation for the invasion, Britain's provost services were not neglected. In July 1940 Traffic Control (TC) companies were formed and these became part of the CMP in the following October. In February 1941, Vulnerable Points (VP) sections were formed for security and guard duties, their Oxford-blue cap covers giving rise to the nickname 'Bluecaps'. The Auxiliary Territorial Service (ATS) had been formed as a women's service in 1938, and in 1942 an ATS Provost was formed. A Special Investigation Branch (SIB) had been formed in 1939 and this body, the army's detective force, was expanded to combat rising levels of theft, fraud, and black marketeering within the military. The theft of war material from cargos prompted the establishment of yet another type of CMP unit, the Ports Provost companies in 1941, while the creation of airborne forces saw the raising of the first airborne provost unit in 1942.

In the Middle East CMP units were involved on the many battle fronts, on the lines of communication to them, and in the maintenance of security at the bases. At the Battle of El Alamein in 1942, for example, L/Cpl. J. Eeles of the 10th Armoured Division Provost Company, won a Distinguished Conduct Medal for clearing a minefield while under fire. MP units frequently dealt with large numbers of prisoners of war, especially after the surrender of 275,000 Axis troops in the capitulation of May 1943. Provost duties on the bases were not always mundane. In April 1944 the mutiny of Greek troops in the area of Alexandria led to weeks of activity before the mutineers were safely caged. Gangs of deserters (with names such as the 'Free British Corps' and the 'Dead End Kids') operated in Cairo and Alexandria, combining with local criminals to steal, defraud, peddle drugs and run guns and ammunition. Countering these activities kept the newly formed SIB very busy indeed.

As the Allied offensive moved into Italy the CMP were called upon to deal with the most serious case of mutiny in the British Army in World War Two. In early September 1943 British and American forces landed at Salerno, meeting with such fierce resistance from German forces that it seemed at one point that the Allies might have to evacu-

Aldershot, 1970s. Until its recent disbandment, the RMP Mounted Troop provided patrols of the camp and training areas. This patrol was photographed as they passed the polo grounds, North Camp. (Private collection)

The first woman Warrant Officer Class 1 of WRAC Provost, 1986. (UKLF)

ate the beachhead. Scarcely had the crisis passed when infantry reinforcement was disrupted by 700 newly arrived men, mostly from the 50th and 51st Divisions, who refused to join any units but their own. After being addressed by a general, most accepted their new postings, but 192 remained adamant and were placed under arrest. They were escorted back to North Africa and tried by courts martial on charges of mutiny. Their subsequent treatment invites comparison with that meted out to British Army mutineers in the Great War. All but one of the Salerno mutineers were convicted. Three sergeants were sentenced to death and the rest received sentences of between five and 12 years penal servitude. The sentences were suspended on condition that the mutineers returned to fight, but most deserted for a second time, were recaptured, and returned to prison. In September 1944 they were pardoned and allowed to rejoin their original units.

In Italy, too, gangs of Allied deserters were at large in cities such as Naples and Rome, creating their own crime waves and taking up much valuable provost time and resources. But most of the effort of CMP units was concerned with the long and bitter struggle as the Allies fought their way northwards. As one infantry officer wrote, 'It is impossible to praise too highly the work of the Redcaps who are part of every fighting division... They developed a tradition of courteous helpfulness which never broke down under the most adverse and dangerous conditions.'

On D-Day, 6 June 1944, the British Army went back to France as part of an Allied invasion of Normandy. Sections of the 6th Airborne Division Provost Company were among the first to set foot on French soil, landing by parachute and glider. Before the day was out several units of Redcaps were ashore, controlling movement on the beachhead and dealing with prisoners of war. Over the next seven weeks 631,000 troops, 153,000 vehicles, nearly 640,000 tons of stores and 88,000 tons of fuel poured into the congested area. Traffic control became a nightmare that absorbed about 80 per cent of CMP resources. As the Provost Marshal of 21st Army Group put it, 'The bridgehead usually looked like a misguided effort to put a quart into a pint pot... But, by the skin of its teeth, creaking and groaning and near chaos, the traffic went, just went.'

In July and August, following a series of bloody battles, the Allies burst out of the Normandy bridgehead. With the enemy withdrawing towards the borders of Germany, the British 21st Army Group raced to secure a northern crossing of the Rhine. By the time increasing German opposition had slowed the advance, British lines of communication stretched back 300 miles to the Normandy beaches, involving most of the available CMP resources in the control of the 1,200 miles of roads that made up the four main supply routes.

Operation 'Market Garden' was an attempt to seize crossings of river obstacles in Holland in order to mount a thrust for the Ruhr, the industrial heartland of Germany. On 17 September 1944, British and American airborne formations landed to capture bridges while a British armoured spearhead drove forward to link them together. At the furthest point in the chain, the British 1st Airborne Division held the bridge over the Rhine at Arnhem. In the battle that followed the 1st Airborne Divisional Provost Company suffered the fate of their parent formation when the armour failed to get through to them. Of the five officers and 66 men of the company only one officer and 11 men were able to make their way back to the British lines. The rest, in common with the majority of their division, were killed or made captive. The Redcaps who controlled the route to Arnhem for the armoured thrust experienced the almost impossible task of passing an entire Corps along a single route under constant enemy harassment.

The failure of 'Market Garden' led to a series of hard-fought and costly battles as the 21st Army Group fought its way through the Rhineland to launch an assault crossing of the Rhine in March 1945. By May the Allies had overrun most of the enemy's heartland and forced Germany into unconditional surrender. In these closing battles of the war, CMP units with the fighting formations were kept busy controlling traffic, manning information posts, and handling prisoners of war, while traffic and the suppression of crime continued to occupy CMP units on the lines of communication. Once again, deserters became a menace – banding together for criminal enterprises and tying down resources dedicated to their capture. With such a large area to cover, policing suffered as black

RMP Land-Rover and 'pointsman' on exercise, BAOR, 1980s. Note his traffic control gear, scarlet beret and 9 mm sub-machine gun. (RMP Museum)

market dealings proliferated, captured enemy equipment was traded, and civilian complaints of looting by British soldiers demanded investigation. In August 1944 the first ATS Provost landed in Normandy, and by early 1945 many more sections were operating along the British lines of communications, dealing with disciplinary matters concerning servicewomen, female prisoners of war, and the custody and search of civilian female suspects.

In the fight against crime in north-west Europe the CMP brought over 36,000 charges, including over 10,000 for absence, 6,409 for offences involving vehicles, 1,249 for theft, 1,092 for drunkenness and 72 for looting. The guilty found their way to one of the series of Field Punishment Centres and Detention Barracks that had been set up in the wake of the advancing 21st Army Group. These establishments continued to be run by seconded officers and staffed by men of the MPSC, assisted by numbers of medically downgraded NCOs, usually infantrymen who had sustained wounds in battle. The regime for soldiers undergoing sentence continued to be harsh, although not as savage as in the military prisons of the First World War. Conscription had brought millions of men into the armed forces, including a number who had followed a life of crime as civilians. The rigours of military life turned others bad, and this core of desperate men exploited the criminal opportunities that war presented by war. Many were very tough indeed, and as determined to avoid front-line duty as they were to commit crime.

An RMP corporal motorcyclist signs a route, BAOR, 1980s. (RMP Museum)

To give up on such men would have been an admission that the dangers of the battlefield were avoidable, so their lives in detention were made extremely uncomfortable. (Though, it was argued, not as uncomfortable as that of an infantryman.) It was official policy from 1941 that, 'In the mind of the ordinary soldier these places [military prisons, etc.] should have a definitely unpleasant association. We cannot afford ... to dispense altogether with the preventative value of deterrence.' Diet continued to be basic, although even this could be restricted as a form of punishment. Hard work, drill and physical training was combined with hours spent in the confinement of cells polishing utensils and equipment. Complaints were made against the staff, with allegations that soldiers undergoing sentences were kicked and punched. The combination of prison populations with an element of hard and desperate men, and the application of such a rigorous regime was explosive. Soon after the end of the war a series of prison mutinies culminated in the destruction of the infamous Aldershot 'Glasshouse' in February 1946. (Many of the men who hurled slates and panes of glass from the roof of the prison at the cordon of Redcaps surrounding its walls, were undergoing long sentences imposed for wartime desertion. They roared their grievances at the crowd which had gathered, which included the author, and these were noted by the reporters

RIGHT **A Redcap on point duty, Germany, 1980s. Note the leather equipment for his 9 mm pistol. (RMP Museum)**

present, who made sensational copy from them. By the time the last of the inmates had been coaxed out of the burning prison it had been reduced to such a state that it was fit only to be used as a store.)

Victory in Europe produced a fresh crop of duties for CMP units. There were over seven-and-a-half million German prisoners of war to be dealt with, millions of displaced persons to be assisted, and thousands of Nazi war criminals to be hunted down. Germany was divided by the Allies into zones of occupation, and much provost time was spent policing the civil population.

In the Far East, Japanese forces advanced into Burma in 1942 and threatened India. The British formations fighting the Japanese were mostly from the Indian Army, in which British units traditionally underpinned Indian units. As an example, one infantry battalion in each brigade was British and all artillery units were British. Following this pattern, provost companies were comprised of sections of British Other Ranks and Indian Other Ranks. The British MPs had powers of arrest over all soldiers, British and Indian alike, but Indian MPs had little, if any, power over British soldiers. This rather odd situation reflected the racial, caste and religious differences that affected the Indian Army at the time. Before the war provost duties in India had been carried out by garrison and regimental police. India had not been a station for the CMP. Provost companies were raised in 1940, and a Corps of Military Police (India), CMP(I), came into existence in July 1942. Rapid expansion followed, with VP and SIB units, prisons and field punishment centres, and a variety of miscellaneous units, dedicated to tasks as wide-ranging as the policing of ports, airfields and prisoner-of-war camps.

It was to take until early 1945 before the Japanese forces in Burma were contained, defeated, and driven out of the country. In addition to the problems associated with the defeat of a tenacious enemy, there were added those of the difficult terrain and climate of Burma, which made traffic control difficult at the best of times, and a nightmare for the provost in the monsoon. After the surrender of the Japanese in September 1945, provost forces played a major part in the reoccupation of former British, French and Dutch colonies, and six provost sections were sent to Japan as part of a British Commonwealth Occupation Force.

The Second World War brought about an unprecedented expansion of provost forces in the British Army. The deployment of large mechanised

Two RMP NCOs merge into the landscape in their DPM uniforms, BAOR, 1980s. (RMP Museum)

forces in campaigns world-wide demanded a growing number of CMP units to control the personnel, vehicles and material necessary to defeat a determined enemy. Officers and men of the Corps of Military Police served in places as far-flung as Norway, the Faroe Islands, Iceland, Gibraltar, Malta, Sicily, Eritrea, Greece, Persia, Iraq, Syria, Lebanon, Madagascar, South Africa and West Africa. In 1946 the effort and sacrifice of the Corps of Military Police in the late conflict was recognised with the granting of the Royal prefix by His Majesty King George VI, the title becoming 'the Corps of Royal Military Police' (RMP).

THE PENINSULAR WAR
1: Lieutenant Colonel Scovell
2: Corporal, Cavalry Staff Corps

THE CRIMEAN WAR/ THE MILITARY MOUNTED POLICE
1: Troop Sergeant-Major Thomas Trout
2: Trooper, Mounted Staff Corps

1855-1914
1: Lance-Corporal, MMP
2: Lance-Corporal, MFP

C

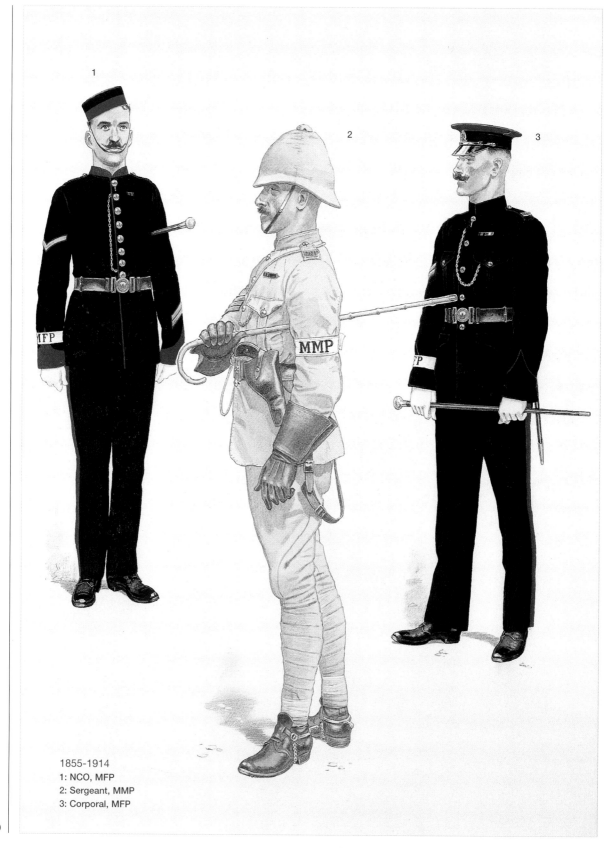

1855-1914
1: NCO, MFP
2: Sergeant, MMP
3: Corporal, MFP

D

THE GREAT WAR
1: Assistant Provost Marshal, Mesopotamia, 1917
2: Sergeant-Major, MMP, 1915
3: 'Garrison Policeman', 1916

E

THE GREAT WAR
1: Lance-Corporal, MFP
2: Assistant Provost Marshal

F

1919-1939
1: Sergeant, CMP
2: Lance-Corporal, CMP
3: Warrant Officer, Class I, CMP

THE SECOND WORLD WAR
1: Captain Sir Malcolm Campbell
2: Private, CMP
3: Lance Corporal, ATS Provost

H

THE SECOND WORLD WAR
1: Sergeant, Airborne Provost
2: Lance-Corporal, 59th Division Provost
3: Sergeant, VP Company

POST 1945
1: Naik, CMP (I)
2: Sergeant, RMP
3: Lance-Corporal, RMP

J

NORTHERN IRELAND, THE FALKLANDS, THE GULF
1: Corporal, WRAC Provost, Northern Ireland
2: Lance-Corporal, RMP, Falklands
3: Lance-Corporal, RMP, the Gulf

K

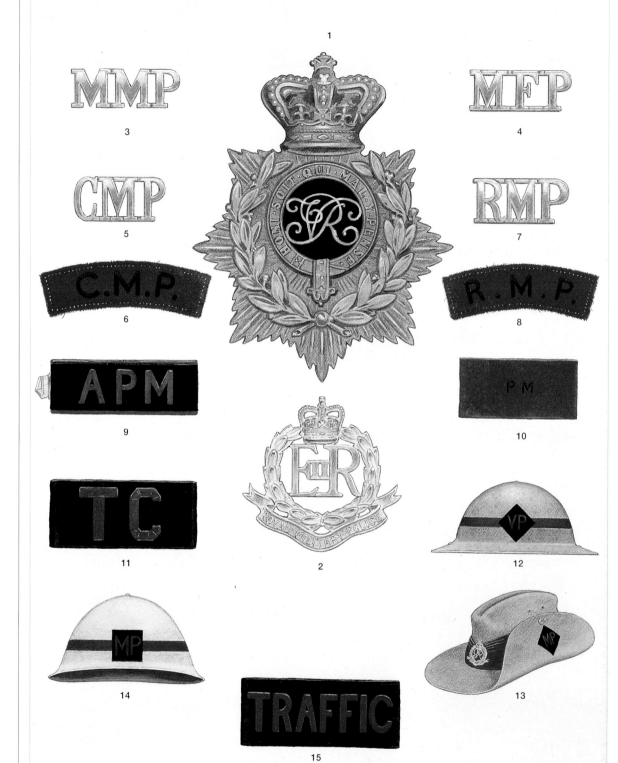

INSIGNIA

THE POST-WAR YEARS

The peace that followed victory over Japan was a short-lived one as far as the British Army was concerned. Unrest in places as diverse as Java, Palestine, India and Eritrea involved British troops in fighting, and by 1948 confrontation with the Soviet bloc had begun, in what came to be known as the Cold War.

National Service

Although demobilisation began in 1945 troop levels remained relatively high in order to garrison overseas possessions and occupy the territories of the recent enemy. The British government decided to retain conscription – National Service – and this was eventually set at two years 'with the colours'. It was extremely difficult to obtain exemption from National Service, and numbers of misfits and ne'er-do-wells were called up for service – most being directed into infantry units. Neither illiteracy nor a criminal record barred a young man from service; the author was a corporal in 1953, and remembers one soldier in his rifle section having 'HM Prison' in his pay-book as a main civil occupation, while he had to read letters from home to another. Most National Servicemen were unwilling soldiers, badly paid, and indifferently housed and fed. Many became expert at 'dodging the column' and making their lives tolerable by scrounging – a euphemism for theft – anything from a mug of tea to a hundredweight of coal. Overseas, especially in Germany in the late 1940s and early 1950s, many supplemented their pay with black market dealings in tobacco, soap, coffee, etc., and smuggled into England the watches and cameras available so cheaply on the continent. In such an atmosphere the criminals in battledress flourished, not all of them of lowly rank. Rackets ranged from the permanent company-orderly-sergeant of a headquarters company who traded the cigarette ration of hundreds of non-smokers, to the staff of an ordnance unit who sold stockpiled vehicles and motor spares. Violence was commonplace, in barracks and out. The Kray twins are probably the most infamous National Servicemen of the time. Called up in 1952 they assaulted the first NCO to shout at them, and graduated from MCE Colchester to the army prison at Shepton Mallet before being discharged with ignominy.

Regiments recruiting from the larger cities often contained elements which make today's football hooligans seem tame by comparison. The soldiers of one such battalion were called 'poison dwarves' by local Germans. Another, banned from every dancehall and *gasthaus* in the garrison, had only the NAAFI club available to them; even there they

An RMP pointsman in NBC suit marshalling military traffic, BAOR, 1980s. (RMP Museum)

fought each other with bottles, sharpened bicycle chains and knives. Assault, murder, theft, sexual offences, robbery in all its forms, forgery, fraud and embezzlement – all these crimes had to be investigated by the RMP (usually by its Special Investigation Branch), and the perpetrators arrested and brought before a court, civil or martial. Whatever the operational roles the provost services had developed in the recent war, they still had much to do in the suppression of crime.

They also dealt with purely military offences, many of which resulted from troops disobeying the 'out of bounds' restrictions placed by the RMP on red-light districts and tawdry bars in an attempt to lessen venereal disease. By far the most common transgressions were absence and desertion. (There was a distinction between the two depending on whether the absconder intended to return to his unit or not.) Many servicemen 'on the trot' from units in Germany made their way to Holland where they lived fairly openly as the protectors of prostitutes. Mutiny was not unknown, although it was usually conducted as a strike against conditions, and never pushed far. There was much discontent amongst the reservists recalled for Suez, with one battalion of a famous regiment striking in Malta. A Territorial battalion, mostly miners, under instruction at an army school, staged a sit-down strike over the poor food being served. A battalion had to be withdrawn from the line in Korea for 'retraining' before going back in with many new officers and NCOs.

The immediate post-war years were difficult ones for the British Army. Overstretched by its commitments world-wide, its ranks filled with unwilling conscripts, and forced to maintain tight discipline at all levels, it depended to a greater degree than ever on an efficient provost service, the junior ranks of which were, of course, National Servicemen. Backing up the machinery of discipline remained the spectre of the 'glasshouse', represented by the many detention barracks, corrective establishments and field punishment centres which the British Army still considered essential. Few who returned from them sinned again. The tales of their treatment undoubtedly kept many more on the straight and narrow.

The Cold War

Whatever the ambitions of the Communist powers, following the defeat of Germany and Japan, they were at first kept at bay by the power of the atomic bomb, but even this failed to prevent localised wars in Asia, where Communist-inspired nationalism confronted colonialism of one sort or another. For the British, a shooting war began in Malaya in mid-1948 when the Malayan Races Liberation Army began a campaign of sabotage and murder. A state of emergency was declared, and emergency powers were adopted. More and more forces were drawn into the campaign until the numbers of troops and

A splendid study of a modern RMP motorcyclist on exercise. (RMP Museum)

police were well over 100,000. Royal Military Police units were kept busy with road patrols and vehicle convoy escorts, cordon and search operations, VIP protection, and some jungle patrolling.

By far the most important role of the RMP in the Malayan Emergency was that of controlling the behaviour of the large numbers of British servicemen who descended on Singapore and Kuala Lumpur in search of rest and relaxation. Their conduct was often bad, especially the infantry-men, whose job in Malaya was hard and dangerous. They arrived at leave centres with the accumulated pay of several weeks and a desire to pack as much living into their four days R and R as possible. What usually happened was that they drank too much and fell out with the 'base wallah' element, who resented the money they threw about almost as much as the jungle warriors resented the safe, sleek lifestyle of the airmen and clerks. Trouble invariably flared over women, and at this stage a Redcap patrol usually appeared, to calm the situation or to pitch in to make arrests. (Serious offenders risked being locked in the Military Corrective Establishment, Kinrara, Kuala Lumpur, a hutted camp on the outskirts of the capital. The author passed through its Stalag-like barbed wire fence in 1954 to deliver up a soldier of his battalion for sentence. There he encountered the MPSC for the first and only time. There is no doubt that MCE Kinrara was, at that time, run as a 'worse option' to life in an operational infantry company.) By 1960 the Communist terrorists had been defeated and the state of emer-gency was declared to be over. The RMP had played an important part in the long and arduous campaign, but it was to be only one of a number of confrontations with forces of Communism.

In 1950 Communist North Korea had invaded South Korea in an unprovoked act of aggression that brought about a rapid United Nations response. This included a large US force and contingents from other member nations, including Great Britain and the Commonwealth. Within months the war became a contest between Communist China, whose 'volunteers' propped up the North Korean state, and the western nations who did the same for South Korea. In time, the two sides fought one

WRAC Provost and RMP working as a mobile patrol, BAOR, 1980. (RMP Museum)

Recent terrorist attacks on British barracks and service families in BAOR have resulted in tighter security. This sequence of photographs demonstrates typical duties of the RMP in this context, checks on vehicles and patrols of vulnerable areas. (RMP Museum)

another across a no-man's-land from systems of trenches similar to those of 1914-18. Fighting went on for three years, and in that time British and Commonwealth forces were formed into a Commonwealth Division. The divisional provost company reflected the composition of its parent formation by having a mixture of Canadian, Australian and British military policemen. A Base Area provost company, operating in Japan and on the lines of communication, was also an integrated unit, with British, Australian, Canadian and New Zealand MPs.

Provost duties in Korea and Japan ranged from the customary traffic control, handling prisoners of war, manning stragglers' posts, and maintenance of discipline, to VIP escorts, airfield security, and operations against black marketeering and vice. A small SIB detachment operated with great effect, and the MPSC helped to run a field punishment centre in South Korea, and an MCE in Japan. In 1953 the Provost Marshal, US Forces in the Far East, wrote, 'I have observed the British Commonwealth Military Police in Japan and Korea, and am proud of my relationship with these outstanding representatives of your service.'

At this time of great tension with Communist China, the garrison of Hong Kong was constantly on the alert for an invasion from the mainland. The downfall of the Nationalist Government, followed by the creation of Mao Tse-tung's Chinese People's Republic in 1949, had made necessary a reinforcement of British forces in Hong Kong, and these included additional provost units. In time, the threat subsided, since when the garrison has been reduced pending the return of Hong Kong to China in 1997.

When Winston Churchill stated that an iron curtain had descended across Europe, he was describing the boundary of Soviet influence, a

RMP Corps Centenary celebrations, 1977. Military police uniforms over the years, with the then Provost Marshal, (Army), Brig. M. Matthews, CBE in the foreground. (RMP Museum)

**Her Majesty The Queen inspecting
sign-making equipment during a
visit to a Territorial RMP unit.
(RMP Museum)**

'no-man's-land' across which East confronted West during the Cold War.
British Forces manned a substantial portion of this line (including part of
Austria and a presence in Trieste) with a main concentration in northern
Germany. Beyond the line, deep into East Germany, a brigade of British
troops formed part of the garrison of Berlin.

By late 1945 the 21st Army Group had been transformed into the British
Army of the Rhine, BAOR, an organisation that has remained in Germany
to this day – albeit much reduced in strength from Cold War levels. The
BAOR began life as an army of occupation, but by the late 1940s assumed
a defensive role as Stalinist Communism began to threaten the security of
the West. Over the years that threat diminished, disappearing in 1989 with
the withdrawal of Soviet forces and the dismantling of the iron curtain.
During the four decades of the Cold War, British Provost forces carried out
a variety of important roles, often in the very forefront of the confrontation
– especially in Berlin. The 1948 Soviet blockade of the city had been coun-
tered by a massive airlift – lasting for almost a year – until rail and road
communications were restored. Control of traffic on the Berlin–Helmstedt
Autobahn Corridor was an RMP task which called for great tact and deter-
mination when dealing with Russian and East German forces. Equally
demanding was the patrolling of the borders of the British zone of Berlin,
especially after the erection of the Berlin Wall in 1961. It was easy for the
most innocuous happenings to escalate into international incidents. The
fact that so few did reflects great credit on the officers and men of the
Berlin RMP units.

BAOR became one of the principal stations of the British Army, involving over 50,000 of its officers and men, and one third of its provost

resources. For half a century the heathlands and ranges of northern Germany have been the training areas of this force, as it prepared for a war that it hoped would never be fought. The RMP controlled the tanks, guns and vehicles as they manoeuvred over the German countryside, year after year, manned by generations of national servicemen and regular soldiers, side-by-side with their NATO allies, and mirrored on the other side of the iron curtain by the forces of the Warsaw Pact. When conscription ended in the early 1960s the British Army became an all-regular service once more. One of the consequences was an increase in the numbers of wives and

RMP vehicle and Sovereign Base Area Police motorcycle, Episkopi, Cyprus. (RMP Museum)

A Redcap and a Royal Naval Provost rating confer, Gibraltar. (RMP Museum)

children accompanying soldiers, especially in Germany. Responsibility for their policing fell, in part, upon the RMP, who recently have had the difficult task of protecting them from terrorist attacks.

Withdrawal from Empire

Confronting Communism went hand-in-hand with the difficult task often described as 'withdrawal from Empire'. Whatever the merits of the British Empire, it was in 1945 a luxury Britain could no longer afford, bankrupt as the country was after two world wars. Not all the withdrawals were peaceful, especially from India and from Palestine. In both countries the British garrisons had contained unrest that exploded into bloody civil war as soon as the last British soldiers departed. In Palestine Jewish extremists had deliberately set out to provoke the British with a series of sickening acts, the worst of which was the bombing of a Jerusalem hotel in 1946 in which 91 people were killed and 45 injured. Two Redcaps shot at some of the 14 terrorists planting the bomb but were unable to prevent its detonation. Up to the time of the withdrawal in 1948, the British forces in Palestine lost 223 killed, including eight members of the RMP.

The Suez Canal zone, Britain's principal base in the Middle East, was subjected to increasing harassment until evacuated in 1956. (The maintenance of the base had required up to 80,000 troops including 11 provost units.) Eight months later British troops went back to Suez as part of an Anglo-French attempt to seize the canal, which had been 'nationalised' by the Egyptians. Redcaps landed with the parachute and seaborne spearheads, ready to direct the main forces in their drive to canal installations, but international pressure brought the operation to an abrupt halt. Within weeks the force had been withdrawn.

The headquarters of the Middle East Land Forces was established in Cyprus after the withdrawal from the Canal Zone. Acts of terrorism by Greek-Cypriots bent on *Enosis*, or union with Greece, had started in 1955 with the bombing of an RMP installation, and these escalated with further bombing and shooting attacks directed against civilians and troops. In the

RMP personnel at pistol practice with 9mm Browning pistols in Cyprus. (RMP Museum)

Bosnia. A group of Redcaps, temporarily wearing the light-blue berets of the United Nations, pose on their Land-Rover against spectacular scenery during Operation 'Grapple 4'. (RMP Museum)

years that followed, the campaign cost the lives of ten military policemen, an indication of the involvement of the RMP in the Cyprus 'emergency'.

In addition to the operational difficulties, the RMP were responsible for the discipline of tens of thousands of troops, to whom most of the island was out of bounds. Off-duty, these men were required to 'walk-out' in groups – armed. They descended upon the few places that were in bounds, and many that were not, creating quite extraordinary difficulties for the Redcaps patrolling red-light districts, bars and cabarets. (Who will ever forget the 'Frolics' in Nicosia, with a middle-aged French chanteuse performing to a mob of howling drunken soldiery until someone fired a burst of Sten into the roof! In the author's unit, a group of off-duty soldiers – including one he had dealt with for insubordination – held up a bar when they ran out of money. When the battalion eventually left Cyprus, the stick-up gang was still in Central Prison, Nicosia.) Cyprus was granted independence in 1959, and terrorism ceased, but the island was to be racked by civil war for many years to come. These disturbances brought to Cyprus United Nations peacekeeping forces, including a provost organisation to which RMP personnel were attached, exchanging their red caps for the blue berets of the UN.

The 1960s saw terrorism erupt in Aden, with most incidents occurring in 1967, the year the British left Aden after granting independence. Once again, the duties of the Redcaps – especially those involving escorts and patrolling – made them vulnerable to terrorist attack. Luckily, they sustained only one slight casualty.

From 1953 to 1956 a state of emergency existed in Kenya as a result of Mau-Mau terrorism. Thousands of British and African troops were brought in to provide security and to hunt down the terrorists, and they caused considerable disciplinary problems for the small RMP forces available, especially in the main leave centres of Nairobi and Mombasa. Particularly unpleasant was the practice of paying prostitutes for their services with rounds of ammunition. The women passed the ammunition to the Mau-Mau terrorists, who might then use it against the comrades of the irresponsible. When caught by the RMP, the culprits faced 'time' in the Detention Barracks at Gil Gil, followed by the retribution meted out by their fellow soldiers on return to their units.

Kenya became independent in 1963, and in the same year Indonesia began hostilities against the Borneo territories of Malaysia. This confrontation lasted for three years and involved British, Gurkha, New Zealand, Australian and Malaysian forces. The RMP units involved found themselves performing a variety of duties including patrolling the few primitive roads, VIP escorts, and duties in aid of the civil police.

Post-war Organisation

During the post-war period, several changes were made in the organisation of the provost service. In 1954 the RMP was authorised to commission officers directly into the corps. Until this time officers had been seconded to provost duties, continuing to wear the insignia of their parent regiment and corps. Over 200 officers were re-badged and transferred to the RMP, and in 1955 the first officer cadet was commissioned into the RMP from Sandhurst.

A sergeant of the RMP guards a UN convoy in Bosnia. (RMP Museum)

The CMP had begun using dogs for security purposes in 1942. The animals had been particularly useful in the Middle East, where they had been used by 'Bluecap' units. After the war the RMP retained guard dog units until 1953 when the animals and their duties became the responsibility of the Royal Army Veterinary Corps. In 1959 the RMP took over guard dogs once more with units in Gibraltar, Malta, Tripoli and Cyprus. RMP Guard dog units were also used to good effect in Kenya and in the Far East. In 1976 the last RMP dogs were handed over to the RAVC ending the Provost association with this type of animal.

Horses had enjoyed a much longer association with the military police. Despite mechanisation, mounted units existed throughout the Second World War and for several years afterwards, mostly in the Middle East and Austria. In 1950 a mounted RMP section was formed in Aldershot, with duties which included patrolling the military lands and town, and taking part in a variety of ceremonial duties and displays. Sadly, this very popular unit was disbanded in 1995.

In 1949 the Women's Royal Army Corps (WRAC) was formed. ATS Provost became WRAC Provost, continuing the duties of maintaining discipline among servicewomen, absentee enquiries, and dealing with problems

MP vehicles – part of IFOR – in the grip of winter, Bosnia, 1996. (RMP Museum)

related to service families. During emergencies, such as that in Cyprus, WRAC Provost were employed to search women suspects, and women and children visitors to detention camps. (The camps – KT and Pyla – contained many hundreds of Greek-Cypriots suspected of terrorist sympathies who were detained under emergency legislation. Visiting was a noisy and boisterous affair, and great care and vigilance was needed in searching food, clothing and books to prevent arms or explosives being smuggled in.)

Northern Ireland

Troops were ordered to aid the civil power in Northern Ireland in the autumn of 1969. (The original soldiers have survived to see their sons patrolling the streets of Londonderry and Belfast, and sadly, may yet see their grandsons employed in the same way.) Among the first were the men and women of the RMP and WRAC Provost who, in common with the rest of the British Army, were welcomed into the Catholic enclaves while the Royal Ulster Constabulary and their B-Specials adopted a low profile. Soon the Redcaps were controlling traffic and investigating civil crime as part of a public protection authority. This honeymoon period was short-lived. In 1970 tension and unrest grew until the IRA decided to take the British Army on. In July, serious confrontation began in Belfast, with the battle of the Lower Falls Road. It left five civilians dead, 18 soldiers wounded and over 300 people in arrest. It also firmly set the Catholic community against the military, a situation that has prevailed ever since.

The emergence of the Provisional IRA was followed in 1971 by the introduction of internment without trial, and in the round-up of suspects the RMP manned holding centres to process the men arrested. (Internment was a political disaster for the British government and had little effect on Provisional IRA sniping and bombing. 43 British soldiers, 16 RUC and Ulster Defence Regiment men, 61 civilians and 52 terrorists died violently in 1971 alone. Worse was to come.) At this time RMP forces in Northern Ireland underwent reinforcement and a 1st Regiment, RMP, was formed, the first such unit in the history of the Corps. The Regiment soon comprised six companies, and contained both provost and SIB personnel.

In 1972 death and violence reached a peak in Ulster. On 30 January, 'Bloody Sunday', 13 civilians were killed in Londonderry by soldiers of the Parachute Regiment. Three weeks later the IRA blew up a Parachute Regiment officers' mess in Aldershot, one of the 1,853 bombings that year, which also included 'Bloody Friday' on 21 July, when a number of bombs were detonated in Belfast causing 139 civilian casualties – including nine dead. The army responded on 31 July with Operations 'Motorman' and 'Carcan', in which 21,000 troops were used to re-enter the Catholic 'no-go' areas of Belfast and Londonderry. These were huge operations and were barely resisted by the IRA. The RMP fielded 20 'arrest and find' teams, 20 investigation teams and a major vehicle checkpoint on the Belfast motorway. Two Redcap casualties were incurred, but with 'Motorman' and 'Carcan' the security forces gained the upper hand in Northern Ireland, and have maintained it to the present day.

In July 1972 a 2nd Regiment, RMP, was formed in Belfast. (The first commanding officer, Lt.Col. B. A. Gait, became the first RMP officer to be awarded the Distinguished Service Order.) Later that year joint RMP–RUC–WRAC Provost patrols began in the city, and Provost forces were augmented by the presence of RAF Police and Royal Marine Police. In time, a policy of RUC primacy was adopted, with the military acting in support of the civil police. In the early days of the scheme the RMP played a major part in its implementation, and, as the RUC began to find its feet, the British Army began to reduce its role, disbanding the 2nd Regiment, RMP, in 1978. In 1985 the 1st Regiment RMP was put into suspended animation. The Redcaps continue to serve in Northern Ireland.

The Falklands War, 1982

The Argentine invasion and occupation of the British Falklands Islands brought about a swift reaction. A British 'task force' was assembled and set sail in May 1982, with an RMP detachment aboard the liner *Queen Elizabeth II*. On 2 June 1982, the force came ashore at San Carlos settlement and began to dig in. An RMP officer recorded, 'The weather is foul with a cold, biting wind, heavy rain… The morale of the boys is pretty good… since we have been in this location we have been attacked by two Mirage fighters… this morning four Canberras came to bomb us but were unsuccessful because two were shot down… Being under attack leaves no room for slow movers.' At first the detachment worked on beach logistic control, marshalling helicopters and manning an information post, but with the advance of 5 Brigade, the Redcaps were employed on close protection of the Brigade headquarters until Argentine prisoners of war started to come in, initially in small numbers, but in a chaotic flood after the enemy capitulation. With great difficulty 11,000 prisoners were disarmed, searched, documented and then put aboard ships for Argentina. In the aftermath of the war the Redcaps had much to do. Property taken from Argentine prisoners was catalogued and civil complaints resulting from the Argentine occupation were investigated. By late July, a joint-service garrison provost unit was established, the original RMP detachment having returned home. Their conduct prompted the Provost Marshal (Army) to state that they 'did a great job in the face of the most daunting difficulties and after the fall of Port Stanley brought order and common sense to a chaotic and potentially disastrous situation'.

The Gulf War, 1991

Following the Iraqi invasion of Kuwait in August 1990, a coalition of nations under the leadership of the United States began to assemble forces in the Persian Gulf. Naval, air and military forces from 35 countries were mustered, initially to prevent further Iraqi incursion, eventually to free Kuwait. The British sent their 7th Armoured Brigade Group, followed by their 4th Armoured Brigade. Eventually these formations were grouped into a newly formed 1st Armoured Division in January 1991.

RMP units were early on the scene in Saudi Arabia, and continued to arrive as the British presence increased. Traffic control and patrolling the base area was followed by preparation for offensive operations as formations went into the desert for exercises and field firing. (It is interesting to note that because Saudi Arabia is a Muslim state, with little or no alcohol available, the drink-related crime that British troops are prone to was at a low level.) RMP provided Close Protection for General Sir Peter de la Billière, the British commander, and a number of visiting VIPs.

Eventually 'Desert Shield', the defence of Saudi Arabia, became 'Desert Storm' as the coalition forces moved to the offensive. The plan of their commander, the American General H. Norman Schwarzkopf, was to feint a frontal attack on Kuwait while mounting a flanking attack to take the Iraqi forces in the rear. The manoeuvre involved the movement of large numbers of men, vehicles and munitions, under the direction of the provost forces of the coalition armies, including the RMP. Over 15,000 vehicles of the British 1st Armoured Division set out on a journey of hundreds of miles to their assembly area, along a route shared with other formations. Traffic control under these conditions was a risky business. Two RMP casualties were suffered before the move was completed, but the deployment was successful and on 24 February 1991 the main ground assault began. A mixed force of Royal Engineer and RMP troops led the British Battle Groups forward,

The Mounted Troop, disbanded in 1995. On the left is Troop Sgt.Maj. E. Scattergood, BEM., Troop Sergeant Major from its formation until 1967. (RMP Museum)

the sappers clearing obstacles and the Redcaps signing the way and controlling the traffic. With the RMP supporting the 7th Armoured Brigade was Staff-Sergeant K. M. Davies, who, discovering that one soldier had been killed and three wounded at a forming-up point, led a group in clearing away 'bomblets', which he did with a shovel. For his action he was awarded the Distinguished Conduct Medal.

By 28 February the Iraqi forces had been roundly defeated, Kuwait had been liberated, and the coalition had ordered a ceasefire. Although the fighting had come to an end, the RMP still had much to do. The prevention of looting and indiscipline were paramount, and there were large numbers of prisoners of war to be dealt with. In the build-up to 'Desert Storm' – considered one of the most complete military victories of all time – the Americans were fond of quoting that 'good logistics is combat power'. The RMP contribution to the mobility of their formations undoubtedly ensured the essential 'good logistics' for the British forces in the Gulf.

The RMP Today

In the early 1990s Britain began a paring-down of her armed forces under a process dubbed 'Options for Change'. In April 1992 an Adjutant General's Corps was formed, and the RMP joined it, losing its status as a separate corps, as did the MPSC who staff the army's last 'corrective training centre'. The Redcaps have been allowed to keep their title, badges, and the famous red cap, and their role remains much the same as it has always been. In the British Army garrisons, at home and abroad, they continue to maintain discipline. In the field they ensure that their formations move effectively. But there are other, newer roles. RMP units were with the first British UN contingents to go to Bosnia, and have remained there through the transition to IFOR. There are Redcaps deployed on the close protection of British VIPs and diplomats world-wide. British military policemen form part of several of the United Nations contingent dedicated to maintaining peace in flashpoint areas such as Cyprus. The present situation in Northern Ireland still calls for large numbers of troops to be held there in readiness against any outbreak of violence, and these include Redcaps. The role of the RMP in the confrontation of any future terrorist threats seems to be assured. With the world in its present state of turmoil, the future of the British Army, and the Redcaps in particular, is guaranteed.

Exemplo Ducemus
(We lead by example)

RECOMMENDED READING

Boyes, Robert, *In Glass Houses* (A history of the MPSC) (Colchester, 1988)

Crozier, Major S. F., MBE, *The History of the Corps of Royal Military Police* (Aldershot, 1951)

Hamblett, J. & Turnbull, J., *The Pegasus Patrol (1st Airborne Division Provost)* (Stockport, 1994)

Lovell-Knight, Major A. V., *The Story of the Royal Military Police* (London, 1977)

Sheffield, G. D., *The Redcaps* (London, 1994)

Tyler, R. A. J., *Bloody Provost* (London, 1980)

THE PLATES

A: THE PENINSULAR WAR

Brevet Lt.Col. George Scovell, 57th (West Middlesex) Regiment of Foot (A1) became Commandant of the Cavalry Staff Corps on its formation in 1813. The CSC never adopted a uniform of its own and Col. Scovell is depicted here in the 'regimentals' worn by the 57th Regiment in 1813. His 1812-pattern shako has an oilskin cover, and he wears the officer's-pattern greatcoat. Before the formation of the CSC, Scovell had commanded the Corps of Mounted Guides, a unit recruited from French deserters and locals. The Guides had some police and intelligence-gathering duties, but were not provost troops. Scovell went on to have a distinguished military career, to gain a knighthood and be promoted to General officer's rank.

To the rear (A2) is a corporal of the 13th Light Dragoons, attached to the Cavalry Staff Corps 1813-14. He wears the full marching order of the 13th. Note the oilskin cover about his light dragoon shako, the red 'provost' scarf worn around his shoulder, his jacket 'buttoned over', and the overalls worn on campaign in place of breeches. The 13th and 14th Light Dragoons earned the nick-name of 'the Ragged Brigade' at this time for their shabby and patched appearance. The corporal is armed with the 1796-pattern light cavalry sword, a pair of pistols in the holsters on his saddle-arch, and a 1796-pattern carbine. His mount's saddle and bridle are of the light cavalry pattern, with the saddle covered by a sheepskin. His cloak, folded and strapped above his holsters, gives the saddle a bulky appearance. His valise is strapped behind his saddle, and attached to it is a coil of rope and a cat-o'-nine-tails, two items essential to his duties.

B: THE CRIMEAN WAR – THE MILITARY MOUNTED POLICE

In October 1855 Troop Sgt.Maj. Thomas Trout of the 7th Hussars (B1) reported for duty at Aldershot with the newly-raised Corps of Mounted Police. He remained with the MMP for 26 years, dying in office in 1881 as Provost Marshal and Commandant of Military Police. Born in 1817, Trout had first seen action in Spain, in the Carlist War of 1836–37, when he served with the 'British Legion', a 10,000–strong army of mercenaries. He joined the 7th Hussars soon afterwards. He is depicted as he would have appeared on joining the new force – a man of 38 years in the undress uniform of the 7th (Queen's Own) Light Dragoon Hussars. Note his badge of rank, (a crown above a four-bar chevron), his pouch-belt and his 'swagger' whip.

To the rear is a trooper of the ill-fated Mounted Staff Corps in 1855 (B2). Swaddled in as much warm clothing as he can find, only his battered helmet – minus its plume – reminds the onlooker of his corps and function. His mount is portrayed in the typical condition captured by photographers of the Crimean campaign. The appearance of horse and rider indicates the effect of the Russian winter on men and animals. Cold weather clothing was late in arriving in the Crimea. The warm coat and boots worn by our subject are typical of the items issued when they became available. His saddle and bridle are the light cavalry patterns of the time. Note the 1829-pattern sword, the pouch belt, sword belt and sabretache. He carries pistols in the holsters in front of his saddle, and there is a whistle and chain attached to his pouch belt.

C: 1855–1914

The mounted figure (C1) depicts a lance-corporal of the Military Mounted Police, Aldershot, in the full dress of the late 19th century. Apart from the red facings to his uniform, he bears a remarkable resemblance to a civilian policeman. He wears the infantry-pattern 'home service' cork helmet, brown leather sling belt and gauntlets. Note his 'MMP' brassard denoting that he is on duty, his whistle and chain worn from his second tunic button, and his badge of appointment (rank) worn on the right sleeve only. His medals are for service in Egypt, 1882. Note also his 1856-pattern saddle, 1860-pattern bridle – both 'universal' patterns – and his 1864-pattern cavalry sword. Military policemen were armed with pistols when their duties required firearms, which was rarely in the United Kingdom.

In the foreground stands a lance-corporal of the Military Foot Police, Aldershot (C2), also in the full dress of the time. This differed very little from that of the MMP, except that the trousers were worn instead of breeches, boots and spurs, and the 'MFP' brassard, which was worn on the cuff in the manner of the civil police. MFP NCOs were occasionally armed with pistols, but were otherwise equipped with sword bayonets. Note the badge of appointment, good conduct chevrons (representing more than five years' service), whistle and chain, brown leather and white gloves. His medals are for service in Afghanistan 1878–80. Full dress would only have been worn on ceremonial occasions. 'Undress', a similar but less elaborate uniform, was the usual form of dress for routine police duty and wear around barracks.

D: 1855–1914

Both the MMP and the MFP chose to wear the cavalry 'pillbox' forage cap as undress headgear in the late 19th century, although the infantry 'Glengarry' would have been more appropriate for the MFP. D1 depicts the undress uniform worn by NCOs of the MFP when on duty in garrisons in Britain.

D2 shows a sergeant of the MMP in the khaki drill uniform worn during the early part of the Boer War of 1899-1902. His cork 'foreign service' helmet has a khaki drill cover, he wears cord breeches and puttees, but otherwise his insignia and equipment is much the same as that worn in Britain. Note his Mark II Webley .455 in. pistol and case, lanyard, shoulder titles and medal ribbons denoting service in India and good conduct. He also carries a cane.

D3 is a corporal of the MFP in the uniform worn in the early years of the 20th century until the outbreak of war in 1914. Still closely resembling the uniform of a civil policeman, the tunic now has patch pockets. A peaked forage cap had, by this time, replaced the 'pillbox', and photographs show this being worn with a red cover over the crown when on duty. Surviving examples show that the first red cap covers were made of waterproof material, painted red. Note his medal ribbons denoting service in South Africa 1899–1902, his brown leather, brassard bayonet and cane.

E: THE GREAT WAR

One of Hollywood's longest-serving 'tough guys' was the actor Victor McLaglen, who specialised in the role of old-time sergeants in John Ford westerns. He served in Mesopotamia in 1917, becoming Assistant Provost Marshal of Baghdad. As E1 he is depicted as a lieutenant APM in the khaki drill uniform worn in Mesopotamia (modern day Iraq). Note his 'Wolsley' topi (sun helmet), Sam Browne belt and .455 in. pistol, APM brassard, breeches, leggings and spurs.

E2 is a sergeant-major of the MMP, 1915. Uniformed completely in service dress, he wears his 'British warm' greatcoat. Note his brassard, badges of rank, pistol and drawn 1908-pattern cavalry sword. His mount carries the standard 1912-pattern saddle and 1902-pattern bridle. In this order military police escorted columns of prisoners of war as they marched to 'cages' in the rear areas.

E3 shows a private soldier garrison policeman in Aldershot in 1916. He wears the insignia of his unit, the 18th Battalion of the King's Royal Rifle Corps, part of the infantry of the 41st Division. Note the brassard of the garrison police, the regimental and divisional insignia worn by the 18th KRRC at this time, and his 1914-pattern equipment. His swagger cane was a popular item with soldiers on provost duties. Between 1914 and 1916 Aldershot became a busy transit camp and training ground for many of the New Army divisions on their way overseas. The camp was crowded and the town teemed with soldiers seeking a good time. Both needed much extra policing – a great deal of which had to be done by garrison and regimental police.

F: THE GREAT WAR, FRANCE 1918

On the outbreak of war the corps of military police moving to France adopted the khaki service dress as worn by **F1**, a lance-corporal on 'point duty', 1918. This MFP NCO demonstrates the items peculiar to the British military policeman of the time. The duty brassard had by now become the item shown, with the legend 'MP'. This was sometimes worn on the cuff and sometimes on the upper arm. The leather brace equipment for the .455 in. pistol appeared at this time, and seems only to have been worn by military policemen. Closely resembling an officer's Sam Browne, it continued to be worn well into the Second World War. Photographs show red cap covers being worn on service dress caps, as well as on pre-war forage caps – which were sometimes worn with service dress. Note our subject's rank badges, good conduct chevrons for more than 16 years service, overseas service chevrons (blue and red) indicating war service since 1914, and the badges of the 30th Division. Note also his helmet and respirator. His medal ribbons are Queen's South Africa, King's South Africa, 'Mons Star', and Long Service with Good Conduct. He is operating a typical traffic control device of the period.

To the rear, **F2**, an Assistant Provost Marshal, on his horse, 1918. The figure is based upon Capt. C. W. Trevelyan, MC of the London Rifle Brigade (TF) who held this post with the 55th (West Lancashire) Division. He wears the collar patches and cap of a staff officer with the brassard of an APM. Note the red rose divisional badge on his sleeve.

G: 1919–1939

Between the wars the CMP saw service at home and abroad, though not in India. Tropical uniform in stations such as Egypt remained khaki drill service dress, worn with the traditional brown leather equipment and a brassard when on duty. A topi was worn during the day, and to this was fixed an 'MP' puggaree flash. (The service dress cap was worn at night.) CMP shoulder titles replaced the old MMP and MFP titles, and the cap badge – which featured the cipher of the monarch – changed with each new reign. **G1** depicts a sergeant of the CMP in tropical uniform, about 1930. Note his badges of rank and medal ribbons denoting service during the First World War.

By this time traffic control had been established as one of the corps' principal roles. **G2** shows a lance-corporal of the CMP

on point duty during military exercises in the late 1930s. By now the white 'sleeves' shown had been taken into use in the interest of high visibility. Service dress was of a smarter cut than that issued during the First World War, and a high standard of turnout was maintained throughout the Corps. By this time the red cap cover was firmly established as the mark of a military policeman on duty.

At the time of the coronation of King George VI, blue 'patrols' were worn by members of the CMP on public duties, and **G3** is a Warrant Officer Class 1 wearing this uniform. Note his badge of rank – worn on the right arm only – Sam Browne belt and 1897-pattern infantry sword, and medals for service in the Great War and long service with good conduct.

H: THE SECOND WORLD WAR

Just before the outbreak of war, an unusual CMP unit was raised by Sir Malcolm Campbell, the famous breaker of land and water speed records. He raised a provost company for the 1st London Division, Territorial Army, by calling for volunteers from the sporting motorcycling fraternity. The response was overwhelming, and Capt. Sir Malcolm Campbell had the company he was to command within a few days. (Renumbered as the 56th (London) Infantry Division, the formation fought in North Africa and Italy.) **H1** depicts Sir Malcolm in the service dress of an officer in the Queen's Own Royal West Kent Regiment in 1939. His medal ribbons are those of the MBE, service in the Great War, and the Territorial Decoration.

H2 shows a private soldier of a CMP traffic control unit on point duty during an exercise in 1941. Note his helmet markings, 'TC' brassard and white 'sleeves'. Note also the insignia on his battledress, which includes CMP titles, the formation sign of Southern Command, and CMP arm-of-service strips. He is armed with a Short Lee-Enfield Mark III rifle, and wears 1937-pattern equipment, respirator and anti-gas cape.

H3 is a lance-corporal of the ATS Provost in 1943. Note the items of military police uniform worn by the ATS Provost with their service dress. These include the red-topped service dress cap of the CMP, the 'MP' brassard, and the whistle and chain. A special 'Provost' title was worn in addition to the brass 'ATS' shoulder title. Note also the lanyard in ATS colours worn on the right shoulder, the CMP badge worn on the left breast and the formation sign of Southern Command. (The latter varied in colour according to the branch of service of the wearer.)

I: THE INVASION OF EUROPE, 1944

Dressed for battle, **I1**, a sergeant of the 1st Airborne Division Provost Company, has the maroon beret of the airborne forces, which has replaced his red cap, and he wears a Denison smock over his battledress. Note his badge of rank and parachutist's wings worn on his right sleeve above an 'MP' brassard to which has been stitched an 'Airborne' title. His equipment is the 1937-pattern webbing and includes a case and pouches for his Colt .45 in. automatic pistol and magazines.

The more conventional appearance of the Redcap of 1944 is demonstrated by **I2**, a lance-corporal of a divisional provost company in Normandy. CMP units began to whiten webbing early in the war, and by 1944 this was almost as much the sign of a Redcap as his head-dress or brassard. Note the 'CMP' blue-on-red shoulder titles introduced in 1943, the divisional sign of the 59th (Staffordshire) Division, and the CMP arm-of-service strip. He is armed with a No. 2 .38 in. pistol.

The 'Bluecaps' were the men of the CMP units raised to guard vulnerable points. **I3** is a sergeant of a VP Company in 1944. His appearance is that of the Redcap of the time except for his cap cover. He is armed with a 9 mm Sten Mark II 'machine carbine' instead of a pistol, and his battledress insignia includes 'CMP' titles, Eastern Command formation signs, CMP arm-of-service strips, and 'VP' badges. His medal ribbons, for service in the Great War and in the Territorial Army, reflect the fact that many older soldiers served in the VP companies.

J: POST-1945

J1 depicts a Naik (corporal) of the CMP (India) serving with the British Commonwealth Occupation Force in Japan, 1946. Note the elaborate pagri head-dress of this Indian soldier and the formation signs of the BCOF on his battledress sleeves including the Union flag. His medal ribbons are those for service in the late war, including the Africa and Burma 'Stars'. He wears an 'MP' brassard and is armed with a .38 in. Smith and Wesson pistol. By this time battledress was worn with a tie.

'Jungle green' replaced khaki drill in some tropical stations during the Second World War. By the 1950s and 1960s it was the standard uniform in Malaya, as demonstrated by **J2**, a sergeant of the RMP. He wears shorts with corps-pattern hose-tops and garter flashes. Note his badges of rank, the formation signs of Malaya Command, 'RMP' shoulder titles and medal ribbons indicating service in Palestine and Korea. He is armed with a .38 in. No. 2 pistol.

J3 shows a lance-corporal of the RMP serving with the 29th Independent Infantry Brigade in Korea, 1951. He stands beside a display of traffic signs typical of those put up by his unit, and one that is not! His equipment is not the usual whitened 1937-pattern, but the 1944 pattern issued to British troops in Korea. ('Oxford' carriers were the tractors used to tow the 17-pdr. anti-tank guns with which British infantry battalions were equipped.)

K: NORTHERN IRELAND, THE FALKLANDS AND THE GULF

K1, a corporal of WRAC Provost in Northern Ireland in the 1970s, is unarmed and wears a 'flak jacket' over her WRAC service dress. WRAC Provost personnel wear a distinctive red-topped service woman's cap as well as an 'MP' brassard. Not visible here is an RMP badge worn on the left breast. (This was a continuation of a practice started in the Second World War, when ATS wore the badges of the units to which they were attached.)

K2 is an RMP lance-corporal in the 'Cold Weather' uniform issued to 5 Brigade for service in the Falklands War. Note the bulky appearance of the DPM parka and over-trousers, caused by the many layers of clothing worn beneath. By this time the service dress cap with its red cover had been largely replaced by the scarlet beret (seen here) and a red-topped No. 1 dress cap. By now, too, the old 'MP' brassard had been replaced by a red item. Our subject wears a DPM brassard to which has been sewn his badge of rank and a patch representative of the 'MP' brassard. Note his 1958-pattern webbing and 9 mm Browning automatic pistol. 'Northern Ireland' gloves and boots complete his uniform.

K3, a lance-corporal of the RMP on point duty during the Gulf War, wears the 'desert'-pattern DPM uniform, helmet cover and special boots issued for service in the Gulf, and a 'shemargh' Arab head-dress worn as a scarf. Note the high-vis-

RSM C. Smyrke, DCM, MMP, 1918. This Warrant Officer's medals form part of the splendid collection of Redcap medals in the RMP Museum, Chichester.

ibility vest worn for traffic-control duties, 1958-pattern equipment, NBC gear and 9 mm sub-machine gun. A brassard on his right arm carries his badge of rank and the formation sign of the 7th Armoured Brigade.

L: INSIGNIA

1: Military Police helmet plate with Victorian crown and cipher. **2**: Present-day cap badge of the RMP – gilding metal for ranks up to Warrant Officer Class 2; silver for all ranks senior. **3**: Shoulder title, Military Mounted Police. **4**: Shoulder title, Military Foot Police. **5**: Shoulder title, Corps of Military Police. **6**: Cloth titles, Corps of Military Police. **7**: Shoulder title, Royal Military Police. **8**: Cloth titles, Royal Military Police. **9**: Brassard, Assistant Provost Marshal, 1914–18. **10**: Divisional staff brassard, 1914–18. **11**: Brassard, Traffic Control, 1914–18. **12**: Helmet markings, VP Companies, Second World War. **13**: Bush hat, CMP (I), Second World War. **14**: Helmet markings, RMP Middle East, 1950s. **15**: Brassard, Traffic Control Companies, Second World War.

Notes sur les planches en couleur

A1 Lieutenant-Colonel par intérim George Scovell, 57e Régiment d'Infanterie (West Middlesex) qui porte l'uniforme "régimentaire" du 57e régiment en 1813. Son shako modèle 1812 est couvert par une housse en toile cirée et il porte la capote des officiers. **A2** Caporal des 13e Dragons Légers, rattaché au Corps d'État-Major de Cavalerie 1813-14 en uniforme de marche complet, qui porte l'épée de cavalerie modèle 1796, une paire de pistolets dans les fontes de sa selle ainsi qu'une carabine modèle 1796.

B1 Sergent-Major Thomas Trout des 7e Hussards représenté en petite tenue des 7e Hussards Dragons Légers (Queen's Own). Notez son écusson de rang (une couronne surmontant un chevron à quatre barres), sa ceinture à sacoche et sa baguette. **B2** Simple soldat du Corps d'État-Major Monté en 1855. Notez son épée modèle 1829, sa ceinture à sacoche, sa ceinture à épée et son sabretache.

C1 Caporal de la Police Militaire Montée, Aldershot, qui porte l'uniforme complet de la fin du XIXe siècle. Il porte le casque en liège de l'infanterie "service national", une bandoulière en cuir marron et des gantelets. **C2** Caporal de la Police Militaire à Pied, Aldershot, qui porte également l'uniforme complet de l'époque. Notez son écusson de nomination, les chevrons G.C., son sifflet et sa chaîne, ses gants de "cuir" marron et blanc.

D1 Petite tenue des sous-officiers de la M.F.P. en fonction dans les garnisons d'Angleterre. **D2** Sergent de la M.M.P. en uniforme de coutil kaki porté au début de la guerre des Boers de 1899-1902. Notez son pistolet Webley Mark II .455 pouce avec son étui, cordon, épaulettes et décoration qui dénotent qu'il a servi en Inde et qui indiquent sa bonne conduite. **D3** : Caporal de la M.F.P. dans l'uniforme porté au tout début du XXe siècle et jusqu'au début de la guerre en 1914. Notez ses décorations qui dénotent qu'il a servi en Afrique du Sud 1899-1902, son "cuir" marron, son brassard, sa baïonnette et sa baguette.

E1 Victor McLaglen présenté en lieutenant de l'A.P.M. dans l'uniforme de coutil kaki porté en Mésopotamie (l'Irak moderne). Notez son topi (casque colonial) "Wolsley", sa ceinture Sam Browne et son pistolet .455 pouce, son brasard A.P.M., sa culotte, ses jambières et ses éperons. **E2** Sergent-Major de la M.M.P. en uniforme de service, 1915. Il porte la totalité de l'uniforme de service et sa capote chaude. Notez son brassard, ses écussons de rang, son pistolet et son épée de cavalerie tirée modèle 1908. **E3** Simple soldat "policier de garnison" à Aldershot en 1916, 18e bataillon du Corps Royal des Fusiliers du Roi. Notez le brassard de la police de garnison, les insignes de régiment et de division portées par le 18e K.R.R.C. à cette époque ainsi que son matériel modèle 1914.

F1 Caporal qui dirige la circulation, 1918. Notez les badges de nomination (rang) de notre personnage, les chevrons G.C. qui dénotent plus de 16 ans de service, les chevrons de service à l'étranger (bleu et rouge) qui indiquent qu'il a servi durant la guerre depuis 1914 ainsi que les badges de la 30e division. Notez également son casque et son masque. **F2** "Asssistant Prévôt", A.P.M., 1918. Il porte les écussons de col et le képi d'un officier d'état major avec le brassard d'un A.P.M. Notez la rose rouge (badge de division) sur sa manche.

G1 Sergent du C.M.P. en uniforme tropical, vers 1930. Un "topi" avec un écusson "M.P." sur le turban était porté durant la journée (le calot de l'uniforme de service était porté le soir). **G2** Caporal du C.M.P. qui dirige la circulation durant les manoeuvres militaires vers la fin des années 30. **G3** Adjudant de 1e classe dans cet uniforme. Notez son écusson de rang (porté au bras droit seulement), sa ceinture Sam Browne et l'épée d'infanterie modèle 1897.

H1 Sir Malcolm Campbell en uniforme de service d'un officier du régiment Queen's Own Royal West Kent en 1939. **H2** Simple soldat d'une unité C.M.P. de contrôle de la circulation en action durant des manoeuvres en 1941. Notez son casque, le brassard "T.C." et ses "manches" blanches. Il est armé d'un fusil Short Lee-Enfield Mark III et porte du matériel, un masque et une cape anti-gaz de modèle 1937. **H3** Caporal de l'A.T.S. Gendarmes en 1943. Il porte le képi à calotte rouge de l'uniforme de service du C.M.P., le brassard "M.P." et un siflet suspendu à une chaînette.

I1 Sergent de la 1e Compagnie de Gendarmes Division Aéroportée en 1944. Il porte le béret bordeaux des forces aéroportées et une Denison par dessus son treillis. Son matériel est en toile à sangle modèle 1937 et comporte un étui et des cacochos pour son pistolet automatique Colt .45 et ses chargeurs. **I2** Caporal de la 59e Division (Staffordshire) en Normandie. Il est armé d'un pistolet No 2 .38 pouce. **J3** : Sergent d'une compagnie V.P. en 1944. Il est armé d'une carabine automatique Sten Mark II 9 mm et ses insignes de son treillis, on retrouve les titres "C.M.P.", les signes de formation des troupes orientales, les galons de la section C.M.P. et les badges "V.P.".

J1 Naïk (Caporal) du C.M.P. (Inde) en service avec la Force d'Occupation Britannique du Commonwealth au Japon en 1946. Il porte un brassard "M.P." et est armé d'un pistolet Smith et Wesson .38 pouce. **J2** Sergent du R.M.P. durant la seconde guerre mondiale. Notez ses badges de rang, les signes de formation des troupes de Malaisie, les épaulettes "R.M.P" et les décorations indiquant qu'il a participé aux campagnes de Palestine et de Corée. Il est armé d'un pistolet No 2 de .38 pouce. **J3** Caporal du R.M.P. servant dans la 29e Brigade d'Infanterie Indépendante en Corée, 1951. Son matériel est le modèle 1944 distribué aux troupes britanniques en Corée.

K1 Caporal du W.R.A.C. Gendarmes en Irlande du Nord dans les années 70. Elle n'est pas armée et porte un gilet pare-balles par dessus son uniforme de service W.R.A.C. **K2** R.M.P. Caporal en uniforme "temps froid" distribué à 5 brigades durant la guerre des Malouines. Notez son sanglage modèle 1958 et son pistolet automatique Browning 9mm ainsi que les gants et bottes "Irlande du Nord". **K3** Caporal du R.M.P. en train de diriger la circulation durant la guerre du Golfe. Il porte l'uniforme D.P.M. modèle "désert", une housse de casque et des protections spéciales distribuées pour la campagne du Golfe ainsi qu'un turban "shemargh" arabe qu'il porte comme un foulard. Notez le matériel modèle 1958, le matériel N.B.C. et une mitraillette 9mm.

L1 Plaque d'identité de police militaire avec couronne victorienne et monogramme. **L2** Badge de calot actuel du R.M.P. - métal à dorure pour les hommes du rang jusqu'aux adjudants de 2e classe, argent pour tous les rangs supérieurs. **L3** Epaulette, Police Militaire Montée. **L4** Epaulette, Police Militaire à Pied. **L5** Epaulette, Corps de la Police Militaire. **L6** Galon, Corps de la Police Militaire. **L7** Epaulette, Police Militaire Royale. **L8** Galons, Police Militaire Royale. **L9** Brassard, Assistant Prévôt, 1914-1918. **L10** Brassard de l'état-major de division, 1914-18. **L11** Brassard, Contrôle de la circulation, 1914-18. **L12** Marques de casque, Compagnies V.P., Seconde guerre mondiale. **L13** Casque colonial, C.M.P. (1), Seconde guerre mondiale. **L14** Marques de casque, R.M.P. Moyen-Orient, années 50. **L15** Brassard, Compagnies du Contrôle de la circulation, Seconde guerre mondiale. **L16** Brassard, Compagnies de Gendarmes Aéroportés, Seconde guerre mondiale. **L17** Badge de calot actuel du Corps d'Etat Major de la Police Militaire

Farbtafeln

A1 Brevet-Oberstleutnant George Scovell, 57th (West Middlesex) Regiment of Foot in der Regimentsuniform, wie sie das 57th Regiment 1813 trug. Sein Tschako im 1812er Muster hat einen Bezug aus Öltuch, und er trägt den Mantel im Offiziersmuster. **A2** Obergefreiter der 13th Light Dragoons, dem Kavallerie-Stabskorps 1813-14 zugeordnet, in voller Marschordnung mit dem leichten Kavallerieschwert des 1796er Modells, einem Paar Pistolen in den Halftern am Sattelbogen und einem Karabiner des 1796er Modells.

B1 Hauptfeldwebel Thomas Trout von den 7th Hussars. Er trägt die Ausgehuniform der 7th (Queen's Own) Light Dragoon Hussars. Man beachte sein Rangabzeichen (eine Krone über einem vierbalkigen Winkel), seinen Gürtel mit Gürteltaschen und seine "Offiziers"-Peitsche. **B2** Kavallerist des berittenen Stabskorps 1855. Man beachte sein Schwert des 1829er Musters, seinen Gürtel mit Gürteltaschen, den Schwertriemen und die Säbeltasche.

C1 Hauptgefreiter der berittenen Militärpolizei, Aldershot, in der Uniform des späten 19. Jahrhunderts. Er trägt den "home service"- Korkhelm im Infanteriemuster, einen Tragriemen aus braunem Leder und Stulpenhandschuhe. **C2** Hauptgefreiter der Militärpolizei zu Fuß, Aldershot, ebenfalls in der kompletten Uniform der damaligen Zeit. Man beachte sein Ernennungsabzeichen, die Winkel für gute Führung, die Pfeife an der Kette, das braune "Leder" und die weißen Handschuhe.

D1 Die Ausgehuniform, wie sie von den Unteroffizieren der M.F.P. (Militärpolizei zu Fuß) getragen wurde, wenn sie in Garnisonen in Großbritannien Dienst taten. **D2** Feldwebel der M.M.P. in der khakifarbenen Drillich-Uniform, wie sie in den ersten Jahren des Burenkrieges 1899/1902 getragen wurde. Man beachte seine Mark II Webley .455 in-Pistole mit Hülle, den Traggurt, die Schulterabzeichen und die Ordensbänder, Dienst in Indien und gute Führung bezeichnen. **D3** Obergefreiter der M.F.P. in der Uniform, wie sie in den ersten Jahren des 20. Jahrhunderts bis zum Kriegsausbruch 1914 getragen wurde. Man beachte seine Ordensbänder, die Dienst in Südafrika 1899/1902 bezeichnen, sein braunes "Leder", die Bajonett und den Stock.

E1 Victor McLaglen als Leutnant abgebildet, A.P.M. in der khakifarbenen Drillich-Uniform, die in Mesopotamien, dem heutigen Irak, getragen wurde. Man beachte seinen "Wolsley-Topi" (Sonnenhelm), den Sam Browne-Gürtel und die .455 in-Pistole, die A.P.M.-Armbinde, die Breeches, Leggings und Sporen. **E2** Hauptfeldwebel der M.M.P. in der Dienstuniform, 1915. Er ist ganz in der Dienstuniform gekleidet und trägt seinen "britisch-warmen" Mantel. Man beachte die Armbinde, die Rangabzeichen, die Pistole und das gezogene Kavallerieschwert des 1908er Musters. **E3** Gefreiter "Garnisonspolizist" in Aldershot, 1916, 18th Battalion des Kings Royal Rifle Corp. Man beachte die Armbinde der Garnisonspolizei, die Regiments- und Divisionsabzeichen, die das 18th K.R.R. damals trug, und seine Ausrüstung im 1914er Modells.

F1 Hauptgefreiter beim Einsatz zur Verkehrsregelung, 1918. Man beachte die Ernennungs- (Rang-) Abzeichen des Soldaten, die Winkel für gute Führung und eine Dienstzeit von über 16 Jahren, die Winkel für Dienst im Ausland (blau und rot), die Kriegsdienst seit 1914 bezeichnen, und die Abzeichen der 30th Division. Man beachte außerdem seinen Helm und die Gasmaske. **F2** "Assistant Provost Marshal", A.P.M., 1918. Er trägt die Kragenspiegel und die Mütze eines Stabsoffiziers mit der Armbinde eines A.P.M. Man beachte das Divisionsabzeichen, eine rote Rose, auf seinem Ärmel.

G1 Feldwebel der C.M.P. in Tropenuniform, um 1930. Tagsüber trug man einen "topi" mit dem Abzeichen "M.P." auf dem Nackenschutz. (Abends trug man die Dienstmütze.) **G2** Hauptgefreiter der C.M.P. beim Einsatz zur Verkehrsregelung während Militärübungen Ende der 30er Jahre. **G3** Warrant Officer Class 1 in dieser Uniform. Man beachte sein Rangabzeichen, das nur auf dem rechten Arm getragen wird, den Sam Browne-Gürtel und das Infanterieschwert des 1897er Modells.

H1 Sir Malcolm Campbell in der Dienstuniform eines Offiziers des Queen's Own Royal West Kent Regiment, 1939. **H2** Gefreiter einer C.M.P.-Verkehrskontrolleinheit beim Einsatz zur Verkehrsregelung bei einer Übung im Jahr 1941. Man beachte die Zeichen an seinem Helm, die "T.C."-Armbinde und die weißen "Ärmel". Er ist mit einem Short Lee-Enfield Mark III-Gewehr bewaffnet und trägt die Ausrüstung des 1937er Modells, eine Gasmaske und einen Gasschutzumhang. **H3** Hauptgefreiter der A.T.S. Provost, 1943. Er trägt die Dienstmütze der C.M.P. mit rotem Oberteil, die "M.P."-Armbinde und hat eine Pfeife an der Kette bei sich.

I1 Feldwebel der 1st Airborne Division Provost Company, 1944. Er trägt das rotbraune Barett der Fliegertruppen und einen Denison-Kittel über seinem Kampfanzug. Seine Ausrüstung besteht aus dem Textilkoppel des 1937er Modells und umfaßt eine Hülle und Patronentaschen für seine Automatikwaffe Colt .45 und die dazugehörigen Magazine. **I2** Hauptgefreiter der 59th (Staffordshire) Division in der Normandie. Er ist mit einem No. 2 .38 in-Pistole bewaffnet. **I3** Feldwebel einer V.P.-Kompanie, 1944. Er ist mit einem 9mm Sten Mark II "Maschinenkarabiner" bewaffnet, und die Abzeichen auf seinem Kampfanzug weisen unter anderem das "C.M.P.-Abzeichen auf, sowie Formationszeichen der Ostkommandos, C.M.P.-Dienstgattungsstreifen und "V.P."-Abzeichen.

J1 Naik (Obergefreiter) der C.M.P. (Indien) in Dienst der Besatzungsmacht des britischen Commonwealth in Japan, 1946. Er trägt eine "M.P."-Armbinde und ist mit einer .38 in Smith and Wesson-Pistole bewaffnet. **J2** Feldwebel der R.M.P. im Zweiten Weltkrieg. Man beachte seine Rangabzeichen, die Formationszeichen des Malaya Command, die "R.M.P."-Schulterstücke und Ordensbänder, die Dienst in Palästina und Korea bezeichnen. Er ist mit einer .38 in Nr. 2-Pistole bewaffnet. **J3** Hauptgefreiter der R.M.P. im Dienst der 29th Independent Infantry Brigade in Korea, 1951. Seine Ausrüstung folgt dem 1944er Modell, das an britische Truppen in Korea ausgegeben wurde.

K1 Obergefreite der W.R.A.C. Provost in Nordirland in den 70er Jahren. Sie ist nicht bewaffnet und trägt eine kugelsichere Weste über ihrer W.R.A.C.-Dienstuniform. **K2** R.M.P. Hauptgefreiter in der "Kaltwetter"-Uniform, die an 5 Brigaden für den Dienst im Falklands-Krieg ausgegeben wurde. Man beachte seine Textilkoppel des 1958er Modells und die 9mm Browning-Automatikpistole sowie die "Nordirland"-Handschuhe und Stiefel. **K3** Hauptgefreiter der R.M.P. beim Einsatz zur Verkehrsregelung während des Golfkriegs. Er trägt die D.P.M.-Uniform in "Wüsten"-Muster, einen Helmbezug und spezielle Stiefel, die eigens für den Dienst im Golf ausgegeben wurden, sowie die arabische Kopfbedeckung "shemargh" als Schal. Man beachte die Ausrüstung des 1958er Modells, die N.B.C.-Gegenstände und die 9mm Maschinenpistole.

L1 Militärpolizeiheitplatte mit der viktorianischen Krone und Monogramm. **L2** Heutiges Mützenabzeichen der R.M.P. - goldfarbenes Metall für Ränge bis zum Warrant Officer Class 2; silber für alle höheren Ränge. **L3** Schulterstück, berittene Militärpolizei. **L4** Schulterstück, Militärpolizei zu Fuß. **L5** Schulterstück, Korps der Militärpolizei. **L6** Tuchabzeichen, Korps der Militärpolizei. **L7** Schulterstück, Royal Military Police. **L8** Tuchabzeichen, Royal Military Police. **L9** Armbinde, Assistant Provost Marshall, 1914-18 **L10** Armbinde des Divisionsstabs, 1914-18. **L11** Armbinde, Verkehrskontrolle, 1914-18. **L12** Helmzeichen, V.P. Companies im Zweiten Weltkrieg. **L13**: Buschmütze, C.M.P. (1), im Zweiten Weltkrieg. **L14** Helmzeichen, R.M.P. im Nahen Osten, 50er Jahre. **L15** Armbinde, Verkehrskontrollkompanien, im Zweiten Weltkrieg. **L16** Armbinde, Airborne Provost Companies, im Zweiten Weltkrieg. **L17** Heutiges Mützenabzeichen des Military Provost Staff Corps.